Success with

Climbers & Creepers

WITHDRAWN

CLAUDIA KRINNER

Series Editor:
LESLEY YOUNG

EHURST

Contents

4 **Foreword**

6 **Plants and climbing aids**

6 Plants for housewalls

6 Buying plants
8 How to recognize healthy plants
8 Where to purchase plants
8 How plants climb
8 Plants that wind
9 Plants with tendrils
9 Plants with roots suckers
11 Ramblers
11 Materials
11 Support sticks
11 Ropes or strings made from
   natural fibres
11 Plastic rope
11 Wire rope
12 Plastic-coated grids
12 Builders' reinforcing mesh and
   wire mesh grids
12 Wood
13 Climbing frames made of metal
13 Planting containers

Nasturtiums are ideal for covering a fence with greenery and flowers.

15 **Creating greenery**

15 A green façade
15 The advantages of greenery on
   a façade
15 Damage to the façade
16 How to avoid damage to a façade
16 The right side of the house
16 Decorative design
17 A green and flowering balcony
17 Doorways and entrances
18 Colour around a window
18 Metal drainpipes as supports for
   climbing plants
18 Climbers on a patio
19 Living fences of plants
19 Covering dustbin shelters, fuel
   stores, etc.
19 Other structures

20 **Position, planting
and care**

20 Planting
20 The right time to plant
20 Position
20 Planting in open soil
21 On a patio
22 On a balcony
22 Types of soil – characteristics of
   soil – improving soils
22 Composts for plants in large
   containers and boxes
22 Pruning
23 The correct way to plant
23 Planting in open soil
23 Planting directly beside a wall
24 Planting in large containers and
   boxes

25 Planting annual climbing plants
26 Care
26 Watering
27 Fertilizing
29 Tying up
29 Pruning
29 Winter protection

30 **Fruit espaliers**

30 Points to note about fruit
   espaliers
30 Growing aids for espaliers
30 Shapes of espaliers
30 Suitable fruit species
30 Planting and care of espalier
   fruit trees
31 The best position
31 The right soil
31 Planting
32 Fertilizing espalier fruit
32 Water sparingly but regularly
32 Tying espaliers
33 Grafting fruit varieties
33 Pruning espalier fruit trees
33 When to prune
34 Training cut
34 A thinning-out cut

34 **Pests and diseases**

34 Damage through the wrong kind
   of care
34 Waterlogging
34 Drying out
34 Nutrient deficiency
35 Clematis wilt
35 Fungal diseases
35 Black spot
35 Pear rust
35 Powdery mildew
36 False mildew
36 Pests
36 Aphids
36 Spider mites
36 Codling moth and sawfly larvae
36 Scale insects
36 Biological plant protection
37 Plant brews
37 Fermented herbal brews
37 Biological plant protection
   agents obtainable in the
   gardening trade

39 **Popular climbing plants
   and espalier fruit trees**

39 Glossary of keywords
39 Key to symbols
39 List of plants
39 Annual climbing plants
39 Perennial climbing plants
39 Espalier fruit tree species

62 **Index**

Kiwi fruit flowers.

Cover photographs
Front cover: *Clematis*.
Inside front cover: *A wall covered in
different kinds of climbing roses*.
Inside back cover: *Virginia creeper
in autumn colours*.
Back cover: *Virginia creeper (top),
honeysuckle (bottom left), flowering
ivy (bottom right)*.

Morning glory requires plenty of sun.

Foreword

Houses and other buildings may be made of concrete and brick but all around them carefully cultivated flowerbeds, patios and balconies and lovingly tended rockeries and hedges bear witness to a human longing to be close to nature. Nowadays many gardens are quite small and patios and balconies do not often provide enough space for all the pots, containers and boxes one might wish. The best way to overcome this lack of lateral space is to make good use of the vertical by allowing plants to grow and flower on a façade and, at the same time, to cover boring buildings, concrete walls and plain fences with greenery. If permitted, in time plants will creep and climb up several storeys, filling the space between a balcony and a roof, above an entrance door and around windows.

This colourful guide will tell you how to make the outside of your house more attractive by using climbing plants. Here you will find a whole host of ideas for greenery to cover any structure.

Author Claudia Krinner, an expert on climbers and garden design, explains which plants are particularly suited to covering a house or balcony with greenery. She supplies detailed, individual instructions on plant care and reveals which plants will flourish both in the garden and also in large containers. Popular climbing plants, like clematis, ivy, Virginia creeper, grapevine, cathedral bell, climbing roses and many others, are shown to full advantage in the lovely colour photographs.

Most plants need some form of climbing aid and in order to help the reader to choose and construct the best one for each plant this volume supplies precise instructions and step-by-step illustrations on the use and securing of the right support. Enchanting flowers in the spring and juicy apples, pears, apricots or peaches in the autumn offer a splendid return for the effort of establishing espaliers. All you need to know about planting and caring for fruits grown in this way against a house wall can be found in a separate, detailed chapter.

To ensure success in the planting of new climbers, the author has provided useful advice on choosing the right position, the best compost and growing mediums, the right way to plant, both in open soil and in large containers, and on watering and fertilizing. Notes are also given on the use of biological plant protection agents, while step-by-step, full-colour illustrations help to convey practical gardening knowledge.

One point that often concerns the amateur gardener is the danger of damage to a house wall or other structure when climbers are grown and the author has covered this topic fully, so that you can feel free to go ahead and cover an entire wall with climbing roses, ivy or a grapevine. Finally, do not forget that "green" walls not only create beauty and a special atmosphere around a house, they also provide shelter and food for many fascinating creatures.

The author
Claudia Krinner has a diploma in landscape gardening and is an expert on garden design and the use of climbing plants.

Author's notes
This volume deals with the planting and care of climbing plants and creepers on the outside walls of buildings. Some of the plants described here are toxic and the instructions for individual care on pages 39-59 indicate this by means of a special symbol. Please make absolutely sure that children and domestic pets are not able to eat toxic plants as they may seriously damage their health.

Also make certain that all climbing aids and espaliers are well secured to avoid the risk of accidents or injury.

A house smothered in luxuriant greenery
Many climbing plants, like the Virginia creeper shown here, manage to cover entire walls in a relatively short time.

Plants and climbing aids

There is no finer sight than a house wall covered by the leaves of a fiery-coloured creeper or enveloped in a mass of green foliage, unless it is a balcony adorned with a colourful, scented cloud of flowers or a patio that is reminiscent of the warm Mediterranean. It may be every gardener's dream but it is an ambition that is easier to turn into reality than you might believe. The range of suitable climbing plants is huge and the right climbing aids are easy to install.

Planting climbing plants around the outside of your home will give it a completely new appearance. The widespread use of climbers can also play a part in improving the general atmosphere of a town and will provide both a habitat and food for many small creatures. Without the need for a great deal of equipment or even special knowledge, you can disguise an ugly corner or adorn the shady side of a building with flowering climbing plants, evergreen ivy or Virginia creeper, covering every surface, from house façades, balconies and patios to above entrance doors and around windows, right through to gutters and composting sites.

Plants for housewalls

The success of your "green" house exterior will largely depend on your selection of the right plants.
Climbing plants: With only a little effort, and in a very short time, some climbers will completely cover ugly façades or large expanses of unsightly wall. Such plants are also suitable for providing greenery on a balcony, on fences and in the garden. One important point to note is that plants have different ways of climbing and will, therefore, require different types of climbing support. Relatively few climbing plants can manage without this.
Fruit espaliers have long been a popular way of growing fruit trees against a wall or fence.
Bushes and hedges: Planted along a fence or the side of a patio, bushes and hedges are excellent for providing shelter or a visual screen. Many species make a home for birds, small mammals and insects and thereby contribute to the protection of nature and encourage wildlife in the garden.
Large container plants are an ideal way of providing greenery in positions where you cannot plant directly into the ground. Many climbing plants are also suitable for planting in large containers or pots.
Summer flowers can be planted in balcony boxes to create greenery and colour anywhere. These are annuals which can be sown as seed or planted as young plants obtained from garden centres or nurseries.

Buying plants

Growing in the right position is particularly important for the healthy development and growth of plants. The mini-climate will vary in different spots so that different conditions will be experienced by plants growing outside, in garden flowerbeds or against a house wall than by plants grown in a large container or balcony box (see p. 21).

Climbing plants which flourish in large containers
black-eyed Susan (*Thunbergia alata*)
cathedral bell (*Cobaea scandens*)
clematis (*Clematis*)*
convolvulous (*Convolvulus sepium*)*
cucumber (*Cucumis sativus*)
hop (*Humulus lupulus*)
ivy (*Hedera helix*)*
kiwi fruit (*Actinidia chinensis*)
morning glory (*Ipomoea tricolor*)*
nasturtium (*Tropaeolum*)
ornamental gourd (*Cucurbita pepo var. ovifera*)
rose (*Rosa*)
runner bean (*Phaseolus coccineus*)*
Russian vine (*Fallopia baldschaunica*)
spindleberry (*Euonymus fortunei*)*
sweet pea (*Lathyrus odoratus*)*
Virginia creeper (*Parthenocissus quinquefolia* and *P. tricuspidata*)
(*toxic plants)

Wisteria will flourish in a sheltered position on the south- or west-facing side of the house.

The most important points to consider when choosing plants are light, temperature, soil and water.

You will find detailed information on the individual requirements of many climbing plants on pages 39-59.

Perennial climbing plants or woody plants do not die back in the winter. Instead, they form woody shoots. These plants are usually sold as young plants in containers or pre-grown in pots. Shrubs can also be obtained as rooted plants and are usually cheaper when bought this way as they do not have a firm rootstock. They may take rather longer to become established than plants bought with a proper rootstock.

My tip: Before planting, make sure that you undo the string securing the cloth around the rootstock so that it cannot strangle the neck of the root.

Annual climbing plants or summer flowers can be pre-grown in pots or bought as seed. They will not survive the winter and will have to be re-sown or bought as young plants again the following spring.

Summer-green, deciduous woody plants (like Virginia creeper), whether bought as a small plant in a pot or with a rootstock and protective covering, are best acquired when they have no leaves. This will help the plant to establish itself more easily as it does not lose so much water through evaporation when it is leafless.

7

Unfortunately, you will not be able to tell at this stage whether you have purchased a healthy, robust plant. **Shrubs** like hops or bindweed, which have a rootstock and have been pre-grown in a pot, are also obtainable in the gardening trade. The parts of the plant that are above ground will die off in the winter; the underground parts will form new shoots in spring.

When purchasing **plants for espaliers**, it is important to consider the height of the trunk of the plant. This is the distance between the neck of the root to the beginning of the crown which is where the plant begins to branch out.

Do remember to note where windows are in a house wall when working out where to plant an espalier.

Climbing techniques
Hops (left) and other winding plants require vertical supports; plants which have adapted their leaf stalks for climbing, like the clematis (right), grow best on grid-like frames.

Climbing techniques
Virginia creeper (Parthenocissus quinquefolia, left) is a plant with suckers. The climbing rose (right) is a rambler which holds on with its thorns.

How to recognize healthy plants
● By their leaves. In the case of large container plants and summer flowers, a good healthy green colour will generally indicate that the plant is not suffering from any deficiencies.
● By the bark which should be completely undamaged. Cuts in the stem that are the result of work done to improve the shape of the plant do not fall into this category. However, any such marks should look clean and some protective tissue should already have grown over them. **Pests and diseases** (see p. 34) should never occur on quality stock.

When purchasing woody plants, remember to check for rust. This is recognizable by tiny, bright red bumps on the bark. Even healthy plants can be infected.

Where to purchase plants
The best place to go is a reputable plant or tree nursery run by professional gardeners. Here, in addition to quality stock, you will also be able to obtain expert advice. You will find the addresses of local nurseries in your telephone directory. You can also purchase a directory of nurseries and plant specialists in most good bookshops, or write to the enquiries page of a reputable gardening magazine (enclose a stamped, addressed envelope).

Garden centres: In addition to offering a similar selection to tree nurseries, good garden centres should also have a large selection of accessories for sale.

Mail order companies also offer a wide selection of plants. Whenever you order something from a catalogue, do make sure that it will come from a reputable source so that you will be certain to receive genuinely fresh stock.

Markets and other venues often offer interesting opportunities to stock your own garden or balcony with new plants, but do check such plants carefully for signs of disease or pests.

How plants climb

Whatever support plants find in nature to help them to climb from the shady ground up to the light, is what you will have to provide artificially around your house or on your balcony.

NB: The type of climbing aid should be chosen to suit the individual climbing technique of the plant. There are plants that wind, plants with tendrils, plants with root suckers and those that ramble.

NB: Various kinds of climbing aid can be obtained to suit these respective climbing techniques (see p. 11). These climbing frames or grids must be fixed to the wall before planting. The minimum space between the housewall and the climbing aid should be at least 10 cm (4 in).

Plants that wind
Most climbing plants belong to the group of winding plants which climb up the support by using the whole shoot. These plants always wind around their support in one direction only, so a distinction must be made (when viewed from above) between:
● left-winding plants which grow anti-clockwise and are most common, and

● right-winding plants (only a few) which grow clockwise, such as hops and honeysuckle.

Climbing aids for winders:
Plants that wind require vertical supports such as sticks, strings or wires.

It is important to choose a support with the correct diameter. Support sticks with a diameter of 3-5 cm (1¼-2 in) are suitable for most winders. A support with a much larger diameter, from about 10 cm (4 in) upwards, would be too big for the winding shoot of *Wisteria* to encircle, for example. If the climbing aids are too thin, on the other hand, very vigorous winders, like Russian vine, may strangle themselves.

Vertical crosspieces between the individual support sticks are merely intended to strengthen the frame and to prevent the plants from sliding down the smooth surface of the support. If you wish a shoot to grow sideways, it will have to be trained and tied (see, p. 29).

Annual winders
black-eyed Susan (*Thunbergia alata*)
morning glory (*Ipomoea tricolor*)*
runner bean (*Phasaeolus coccineus*)*

Perennial winders
Akebia quinata
*Celastrus orbiculatus**
Dutchman's pipe (*Aristolochia macrophylla*)
honeysuckle (*Lonicera*)*
hop (*Humulus lupulus*)
kiwi fruit (*Actinidia chinensis*)
Russian vine (*Fallopia baldschaunica*)
wisteria (*Wisteria sinensis*)*

(*toxic plants)

Plants with adhesive pads and root suckers
Virginia creeper (Parthenocissus tricuspidata "Veitchii", left) climbs with the help of adhesive pads; ivy (right) uses root suckers.

My tip: Winders require enough space to encircle their support. Wall spacers (see illustration, p.13) will ensure the necessary gap between the wall and the frame (minimum distance 30 cm (12 in).

Plants with tendrils
These plants climb by using specially adapted organs, for example, either with the help of specially adapted long leaf stalks, like the clematis (*Clematis*), or by using tendrils which evolved through an adaptation of the shoots, as in the case of the grapevine (*Vitis vinifera*).
There are:
● plants which climb by means of long leaf stalks that are sensitive to pressure
● plants with suckers, which use their slender shoots purely for climbing
● plants with tendrils, which have developed additional adhesive pads on the tips of their shoots to help them to climb without any other kind of aid. These include some forms of Virginia creeper (*Parthenocissus tricuspidata* "Veitchii" and *Parthenocissus quinquefolia* "Engelmannii") which only grow a few adhesive pads.

When stimulated by pressure or touch, these pads secrete minute quantities of an adhesive which hardens on exposure to air.

Climbing aids for plants with tendrils: Net or grid-shaped climbing aids made of wood, wire, strings or builders' reinforcing mesh. Grids, wire mesh and wires may be arranged vertically, horizontally or even diagonally.
● The individual sticks of a grid or frame should not be too thick as the tender shoots would find it too difficult to wind around them.

Annuals with tendrils
cathedral bell (*Cobaea scandens*)
nasturtium (*Tropaeolum majus, T. peregrinum*)
ornamental gourd (*Cucurbita pepo var. ovifera*)
sweet pea (*Lathyrus odoratus*)*

Perennials with tendrils
clematis (*Clematis*)*
grape vine (*Vitis vinifera*)
Virginia creeper (*Parthenocissus quinquefolia, P. tricuspidata*)
(*toxic plant)

● In the case of delicate plants, for example those that use extended leaf stalks, like nasturtium, the mesh gauge of a grid should not be more than 5 x 5 cm (2 x 2 in).

Plants with root suckers
Plants may also climb with the help of their roots, for example ivy. As soon as it comes into contact with a firm base, ivy produces special adhesive roots straight out of the shoots just beneath a leaf stalk.
Being "true climbing plants", plants with root suckers do not require any kind of climbing aid.

My tip: Young plantlets like to use a short piece of string or a stick leaning diagonally against the wall as a means of getting started in the right direction.

Ramblers

Ramblers like the climbing rose (*Rosa*) are not equipped with specially adapted climbing organs. Instead, they produce long, flexible shoots, usually also equipped with thorns or prickles, to help them to climb up the larger supporting plants that they hold on to. If they cannot find enough support themselves or their own weight pulls them down, however, it will be necessary to supply them with additional climbing aids.

Honeysuckle covering an arch
This vigorous climber soon covers an arched climbing frame with a profusion of summer flowers.

Climbing aids for ramblers: Use grids or frames with as many vertical battens as possible, for example, diagonal grids. These plants cannot climb by themselves so their new shoots have to be woven into the frame or tied up from time to time.

Materials

As a rule, erecting climbing aids is not something for which you will need planning permission but it is always a good idea to ask your landlord if you are renting a home. The case is different if the building is listed and this point should be checked with the relevant authority.

Support sticks

Support sticks made of wood, plastic, metal or plastic-coated metal are among the simplest types of climbing aid. They can be arranged in a pattern or woven together with the help of wire or string, or you can stand several sticks in such a way that they meet at the top.
Use: These are ideal for winding plants, like runner beans, black-eyed Susan or Russian vine.
Securing: Lightweight sticks for supporting annual winders should be driven about 50 cm (20 in) deep into the soil. More stable sticks can be set in holes 50-80 cm (20-32 in) deep, perhaps even cementing them in if they are intended to

support very vigorously growing climbing plants like Russian vine. Drive the sticks into the compost in a pot or large container if the plants are to grow in pots.

Ropes or string made from natural fibres

Ropes made of hemp, sisal or coconut fibre can be obtained in the gardening trade. They are plant-friendly and provide a firm grip as they have a rough surface. Their durability will be somewhat limited, however, if they are used outdoors. They also tend to expand in increased humidity so the support they give to the plants can end up being too loose.
Use: For annual winders.
Securing: Knot them to screw-in eyes or to rings that can be dowelled into the housewall.

Plastic rope

It is essential to use string or rope with a rough surface as a climbing aid in order to prevent the plant from sliding down. Nylon hop ropes, 1.5 mm thick, can be obtained in the trade. These ropes have a rough surface, are cheap, can be straightened out quite easily with a simple stretcher (obtainable from hardware shops) and will last a long time.
NB: Vigorously growing winders may become too heavy for these ropes.
Use: For perennial winders like kiwi fruit and hops.
Securing: Fasten them to the housewall in the same way as rope made of nylon (see above).

Wire rope

Because of their strength, wire ropes can be used to bridge larger gaps. Galvanized or plastic-coated stainless steel wire will have sufficient anti-rusting qualities.

To prevent winders from sliding down smooth surfaces of vertical supports, provide horizontal supports, install screw-on wire rope clamps at regular intervals to act like "knots", or rough up the plastic coating.

Use: For winders like hops and Dutchman's pipe.

Securing: These must be fixed securely because of the load on the support. A tripod dowelled into the wall at the top end of the rope/wire should be sufficient. Anchoring the rope/wire in the soil can be achieved with the help of a point anchor made of concrete or heavy, galvanized metal plates. Use metal eyelets that have been cast in, welded on or screwed on (see illustration above).

Use various kinds of stretchers to pull the rope taut (obtainable in the trade or from hardware shops; remember to indicate the gauge of wire you are using):

● simple wire stretchers for ropes less than 3 m (10 ft) long; these can only be tightened by a maximum of 25 cm (10 in)

● locking stretchers for use with thicker wire and rope to a length of over 3 m (10 ft). Thinner rope ends should be tidily twisted together using pliers at the junction point with the stretcher. Thicker wire ropes are best taken to a professional ropemaker where the ends of the rope are placed in soft metal capsules and then sealed together under great pressure.

Plastic-coated grids

The gardening trade can supply a good stock of plastic-coated metal grids and plastic-coated metal wire, including tools, as ready-to-buy items. They are easy to assemble and are normally treated against rusting by the manufacturers.

Uses: For plants with tendrils and

Fixing wire supports
At the top end, a tripod has been dowelled into the wall (left). A point anchor made of concrete is used to anchor the wire into the ground.

winders like *Clematis* or smaller climbing roses. These grids would rapidly end up being too small for vigorously growing plants like *Wisteria* or Russian vine.

Securing: Hang on wall spacers with dowelled wall hooks (see illustration, p. 13)

Builders' reinforcing mesh and wire-mesh grids

Builders' reinforcing mesh can be bought in sections of 2.5 x 5 m (8 x 17 ft) in builders' suppliers. Use a strong metal saw or a bolt cutter for cutting the mesh to size. This mesh is easy to shape into arches or pergolas or to fix to walls as a flat climbing aid. Note that it will need a coat of anti-rust paint.

Wire-mesh frames are also suitable as climbing aids. The wire mesh is very cheap and is usually galvanized. It will be even stronger if it is set into a strong wooden frame and fixed with U-shaped steel nails (see illustration, p. 13).

Use: For winders like *Clematis*, sweet peas or nasturtiums.

Securing: Install in the same way as plastic grids (see above).

Wood

Wooden frames or grids are still the most popular element for

supporting green climbing plants because of their natural look, plant-friendly qualities and the multitude of possibilities for use.

Use: For perennial winding plants and plants with tendrils.

My tip: The diameter of wooden battens may sometimes be too large and additional horizontal strings or thinner wooden battens will have to be provided as climbing aids.

NB: Climbing frames made of wood should not be in direct contact with the soil which might cause the wooden parts to start to decay from the bottom up (it is a good idea to secure them in concrete with a "metal shoe").

Wood protection agents:
Treating the wood with a protection agent before installation is recommended. Try to use biological wood protection agents as they are less harmful to humans and plants. Such agents include: linseed oil, wood oil, wood tar, soda and natural resins. You can also obtain pigments (in powder form) for mixing with the agent to obtain a colourful finish.

Pressure-treated woods (the protection agent is driven into the wood under high pressure) are good for use as posts or weight-bearing supports with a larger diameter. They should not, however, contain substances that are harmful to plants, such as phenols, chlorine or ammonium hydroxide. When purchasing wood, ask which agents have been used to treat it.

The most important points to remember when using wood are:

● Use high quality wood with few knotholes.

● Cover up exposed ends with plastic or metal strips to protect them against rain.

● The use of planed wood will decrease the risk of the wood becoming soaked right through.
● The unprotected ends of posts should be cut off at an angle so that water can run off more easily.

Grids made of wood: These can easily be made out of roof battens which can be obtained from a timber yard or builders' merchant in a range of diameters from 2 x 4 cm (¾-1½ in) to 4 x 6 cm (1½-2½ in) and in lengths of about 2-6 m (7-20 ft), either rough cut or planed, in a natural, untreated state or pressure-treated. Even without any previous experience of woodwork, you will find them easy to assemble into the desired grid pattern and they are very cheap to buy. When constructing a wooden grid, nail, screw or glue the battens together both horizontally and vertically. Use rustfree wire pegs or a weatherproof glue or screws.

Securing: Use dowels for fixing hooks into the wall. Use metal or plastic capsules as spacers. Pieces of cork will do equally well if the spaces are small.

Climbing frames made of metal

Metal structures, made from steel pipe, for example, and properly treated against rusting, are very durable and strong. They are especially useful for creating free-standing, three-dimensional or curved climbing frames.
It will be necessary to tie the plants on. Such elaborate climbing frames will have to be made in a metal workshop.

Use: For rose arches, gateway arches, bowers and covered walks; for annual and perennial climbing plants, plants with tendrils and ramblers.

Securing: This should be carried out by the manufacturer.

Planting containers

Fortunately, many climbing plants do not make great demands with respect to space, so they will flourish just as well in large containers, pots and balcony boxes.
The most important points to consider when choosing plants are:
● All containers, no matter what material they are made of, must be equipped with drainage holes so that excess water can run away. Very few plants can cope with waterlogging.
● All large plant containers require a drainage layer (see illustration, p. 23).
● Containers for climbing plants must be sufficiently spacious as the plant will require plenty of room for the development of its roots if it is to produce large amounts of leaves and flowers. Annuals will make do with an ordinary balcony box but perennials require a container that is at least 30-40 cm (12-16 in) deep, and wide enough to leave space for an insulating layer made of polystyrene (see winter protection, p. 29).
● Before purchasing any large, heavy containers, troughs or urns, find out the carrying capacity of

your balcony or patio. Even if the plants themselves are not that heavy, the weight of the containers increases dramatically when filled with wet compost.

Clay containers: The porous material from which these containers are made makes an exchange of air possible among the roots of the plant and the risk of waterlogging is also reduced as excess water can evaporate through the walls of the vessel. On the other hand, rapid evaporation will also cause the soil to cool quickly around the roots, which many plants dislike. Clay pots and containers are not suitable for overwintering outside.

My tip: Before using them, clay and terracotta pots should be soaked in water long enough so that no more tiny air bubbles are seen rising to the surface. This means that the clay is now saturated with water and, to begin with at least, chalky deposits will be avoided. When they do appear, scrub them off with a tough scrubbing brush and a vinegar and water solution (1:4).

Wooden containers:
● Always stand wooden containers on a base to prevent the rapid decay of the wood.

A wire grid with a wooden frame

Lay the wire mesh on the wooden frame (left), use U-shaped nails to fix the edge of the wire (centre) and hang up the frame using spacers (right).

13

Nasturtiums quickly produce a mass of colourful flowers on a fence.

Black-eyed Susan is a very undemanding summer-flowering plant.

● Wooden containers are subject to weathering. Make sure they have been painted inside and out with a plant-friendly wood protection agent (see p. 12).

Plastic containers: The advantages are fairly obvious. They are cheap to buy, longlasting, do not weigh much and are, therefore, ideal for balconies and windowsills. They are also practical and easy to clean as the smooth surface will not encourage the growth of algae.

Troughs made of natural stone: Usually, no drainage holes have been provided so the container will require a good drainage layer (see p. 24). Carefully choose the position in which you are going to keep the trough as its weight will prevent it from being moved about too easily.

Plant containers with a water reservoir: Recently, the gardening trade has introduced plant containers with inbuilt water reservoirs. The reservoir is at the bottom of the plant container and, depending on the size of the container, can hold up to 10 litres (17½ pt) of water. Fertilizer can also be introduced in this way.

NB: These containers should also be equipped with a properly functioning water-level indicator. Too much water in the container would cause the roots to rot as they would be standing in water all the time. Even when using this method, you will not be able to dispense with watering for more than a few days as plants in large containers will require lots of water, particularly if they are placed in a sunny position.

Creating greenery

Walls covered in green foliage are not only an aesthetically pleasing adornment of houses and other buildings in towns and villages, they also provide a habitat for birds and other wild creatures. In this way, foliage and flowering plants, grown against a house wall or in pots and containers, can be used to create a natural haven all around the outside of your house.

A green façade

Before buying plants to cover a wall you should give some thought to what you intend to achieve.

● Will you wish to influence the direction in which the plants grow or do you not mind which way they climb up the wall? You could choose climbing plants which require climbing frames that merely need fixing to the wall in the right position for the plant to cover the wall with greenery. Or you may wish to allow plants with root suckers, which do not require any climbing aids, to grow unhindered up a wall.

● Do you want the wall to be covered in greenery as soon as possible and up to what height do you wish the plants to climb? Hops and Russian vine, for example, are recommended as fast-growing climbers; ivy and spindleberry (*Euonymus fortunei*) are much slower, at least for the first few years.

● If you wish to cover the entire façade with a uniformly dense, green tapestry, the best plants are ivy and Virginia creeper. If, however, you wish only part of the façade to be hidden or even a particular area of it, for example to emphasize the importance of the entrance, clematis, roses, Dutchman's pipe and honeysuckle would be most suitable.

The advantages of greenery on a façade

Houses covered in climbing plants are not only ecologically beneficial, they also profit from many favourable effects created by the woven covering of plants. Plants growing on a wall provide a kind of protective covering for the house.

A habitat for birds and insects: Green façades create new living spaces which offer many creatures shelter and nesting facilities and also food in the shape of flowers and fruit. In addition to bees, beetles, butterflies and spiders, birds and bats will also join the community on the house wall, where both prey and predators will feel at home.

A temperature equalizer: Plants allow water to evaporate through their leaves. This process leads to a slight cooling in temperature of their immediate surroundings, which is why outdoor seating in many warm countries is often surrounded by climbing plants.

Due to this effect, houses covered in greenery enjoy a more temperature climate. The temperature is lowered slightly in hot summer weather, while the cold of winter is alleviated a little by an evergreen plant covering. The difference in the daytime and night-time temperature is also decreased.

Protection from rain and weather: A thick plant covering will protect a house wall from rain. There is still plenty of ventilation behind the protective covering of leaves, so the wall will not be covered in condensation. Thickly covered house walls will be shielded even from heavy showers.

Increase in humidity: Plants on a house wall lose water through evaporation to the immediate environment without the moisture condensing on the wall.

Damage to the façade

Very often, damage to a house wall is ascribed to climbing plants which are not the culprits at all. Instead, already damaged or damp masonry is responsible for the problems. The reputedly damaging effect of ivy or Virginia creeper on a façade just does not happen so long as the façade was undamaged to begin with as the adhesive pads and roots will not harm sound rendering or cement. Plants with tendrils and adhesive pads, like Virginia creeper, secrete a sticky substance to allow them to adhere to the wall and this does no damage to the wall. Climbing plants never bore holes or make cracks in walls, they only take advantage of already existing uneven places and cracks. This means that damaged walls should be properly repaired before allowing plants to climb up them.

Grown in a sunny position, a Virginia creeper will produce beautifully coloured autumn foliage.

How to avoid damage to a façade

● Ivy or Virginia creeper should not be planted right beside wooden walls that require regular painting. Old sheds or garage walls will suit these plants.

● Façades treated with water-repellent paint are not suitable for plants with root suckers. The root suckers of ivy may penetrate the top layer of paint and continue producing roots underneath this. The consequence will be peeling paint.

● Gutters and the surfaces of roofs should not have plants climbing across them. Self-climbing plants on roof surfaces will push their shoots under the roof tiles and even lift them up.

NB: Gutters that are blocked with growing plants will lead to dampness in walls.

The right side of the house

Different plants have different requirements as to position. The section on care (see p. 39-59) will tell you which side of the house is suitable for which plants.

The south-facing side: This is the ideal position for kiwi fruit, grapevines or espalier fruit (the south-facing side is too warm for apples) and deciduous climbing plants like wisteria, roses, honeysuckle or morning glory.

The west-facing side: This is often the side which receives most rain in northern Europe, although it also enjoys the full warmth of the afternoon sunshine and can therefore support espalier fruit. A dense, evergreen covering will protect the fruit against heavy rain.

The east-facing side: Here, the morning sun will still provide enough warmth for active growth and this side is also often more protected than the west-facing side. However, late frosts in spring may damage the flowers of espalier fruit on this side, which may mean a lack of fruit later on.

The north-facing side: Here, it is better to plant evergreen plants which cover the whole surface, like ivy. The north-facing side is not suitable for planting espalier fruit.

Decorative design

Deciding to cover your house with greenery will still leave plenty of scope for your own ideas, whether this is the choosing and combining of different plants, the building of suitable climbing aids or the optimal utilization of existing surfaces.

Climbing roses and Virginia creeper.

The autumn colours of Virginia creeper.

A green and flowering balcony

A sufficient screen from neighbouring balconies can be obtained with tall-growing climbing plants like runner beans which can be trained on simple strings or wires (see p. 11). (Always check about attaching fixtures with your landlord.) Green and flowering climbing plants on horizontal wires or strings will transform your balcony into a densely covered, flowering summer bower. Annual winders and plants with tendrils are most suitable for this and will manage quite well in flowerboxes or pots. Charming contrasts can be created with a combination of climbing plants and annual summer flowers in a pot. Perennial species (in containers with a height of at least 35 cm/14

in and a diameter of 30-40 cm/ 12-16 in) which need to overwinter on a balcony, should be hardy.

Make sure to consider the following points when establishing plants on a balcony:

● Balconies that are open to strong winds require protection from the wind to allow young plants to acclimatize themselves; for example, by using bamboo matting as a screen.

● Plants on a balcony are more susceptible to attack by pests which means more time spent on care.

● Boxes fixed to the outside of a balcony railing must be secured properly.

Doorways and entrances
You can create greenery around your entrance door with

honeysuckle, Russian vine and Virginia creeper – sometimes these plants will end up supplying a covering of greenery over the entire façade. The way to set plants directly into the soil beside a doorway is shown on page 22. A green archway above an entrance doorway, for example in the garden of a terraced house, can be covered with roses, honeysuckle or clematis. Large container plants, like bay and box trees, can look very charming beside a rather grander doorway. Climbing plants can also be trained on frames or taut wires (see pp. 11 and 12) on both sides of a doorway, and may be planted in large containers or boxes. The entrance to a house may not always be in a sheltered position, so only choose plants that are not too sensitive to wind and weather.

Colour around a window

Windows can be transformed into mini-balconies.

● If there is an outside window ledge, you can utilize the depth and width of the embrasure and stand a box on the ledge. Secure it well, so that it cannot tip off!

● Use lightweight boxes as window ledges cannot cope with a great amount of weight.

● Never install windowboxes on the side of the house that is most exposed to wind or rain.

● Hardy, perennial climbing plants, like ivy or clematis, may be allowed to cover a façade from a window by using sufficiently insulated windowboxes (see winter protection, p. 29). Draw taut wires or strings along the wall beside the window to provide a climbing frame for the plants. These supports should be secured to the wall with wall hooks that have been dowelled in. Make sure to check with your landlord first.

Metal drainpipes as supports for climbing plants

If a vertical drainpipe is anchored properly and is a sufficient space out from a wall, it may be used as an ideal support for less hefty winding plants like Dutchman's pipe, hops, black-eyed Susan or runner beans. Wisteria, for example, should never be allowed to climb up a drainpipe; its metre-long shoots will become woody and tough in time and are quite capable of "strangling" a drainpipe. Very delicate winding plants, on the other hand, will not be able to use such large pipes.

● If no place for planting is available at the foot of a drainpipe, you can create a planting pit (see p. 23) or set the plants (preferably annuals) in a pot or container.

Clematis alpina "Francess Rivis".

● In order to prevent the shoots from slipping down the smooth surface of a drainpipe to begin with, you may carefully tie the plant to the pipe or draw a hop string from the ground to the top. **NB:** Remember to cut the plant back so that it cannot block the top of the drainpipe.

My tip: Do not allow plants with tendrils and adhesive pads to climb up drainpipes and do not plant them near pipes as their adhesive pads tend to create rust spots on metal surfaces. Plastic drainpipes should not be used for climbers as they will not bear the weight.

Climbers on a patio

A patio will provide plenty of room for a multitude of different combinations of plants.

Large container plants, like oleander, bougainvillea or hibiscus, will feel particularly at home on a patio on the south-facing side of the house. (Advice on growing plants in large containers is given on pp. 20-9.)

Climbing plants on patios or fences can turn boring party walls or wire fences between adjoining gardens into a living screen.

● Honeysuckle, clematis or roses, planted in beds beside patios or along walls, will produce a riot of summer flowers, particularly if planted in a south-facing position.

● If you want to hide a patio wall or an adjoining wire fence with a covering of green foliage even in winter, the best species to plant are ivy or *Euonymus fortunei* which will also flourish on a north- or east-facing patio.

Clematis montana "Rubens" is a profusely flowering variety.

● If there is no room on a house wall, perennial climbing plants can be grown in a large trough in front of a patio wall.
Simple builders' steel mesh or strings that have been secured to wall hooks will be sufficient as a climbing aid (see p. 12).
Shrubs will also provide a wonderful visual screen beside a patio or along a fence. Hedge maple, lilac, forsythia or spiraea will provide cheerful accents with their flowers, fruit or colourful autumn foliage. Most shrubs will require planting in open soil on account of their size and the extent of their root systems.

Fences
If you do not have enough room for a proper hedge, fences constructed of different materials, such as wire or wood, are absolutely ideal as climbing aids.

Climbing plants will produce enchanting flowers in the summer and Virginia creeper will decorate your fence with a wealth of wonderful, glowing-red leaves in the autumn.
● Vertical fence posts are ideal for supporting winding plants like convolvulous, black-eyed Susan or morning glory. Any missing horizontals needed can easily be added by drawing rope or wires from post to post.
● Plants with tendrils, like nasturtium, clematis or sweet peas, will climb effortlessly on small-gauge wire fences.
● Using annual plants, you can create a different look along a fence every year and also have the time to provide wooden posts with a regular protective coat of paint.
● Vigorously growing perennials, like wisteria or hops, require a fence height of at least 2-2.5 m

(7-8 ft). The fence must also be very strong.
● You can find out just how many plants you will require for your length of fence, and the proper spacing of these plants, on pages 39-59.
● Plantations of shrubs or other plants along fences not only provide an attractive visual screen, they are also high on the list of ecologically beneficial improvements: hazelnut, hedge maple or cornelian cherry (*Cornus mas*) provide shelter and food for birds and small mammals like hedgehogs or dormice.
NB: Make sure there will be enough space between your plants and any neighbouring property when planting beside fences. Find out how large the plants will grow when you buy them.

Covering dustbin shelters, fuel stores, etc.
Even such unattractive objects as these can be use to support plants if you choose the right ones.
● Virginia creeper will soon obscure dustbin shelters and other structures. Ivy will also cover such ugly eyesores with its green foliage but will do better in less sunny positions.
● Instead of going for a complete covering, you could also stand plant troughs of summer flowers, like busy Lizzy, pinks or daisies, or climbing plants with hanging shoots, like Virginia creeper (*Parthenocissus quinquefolia*), on top of a dustbin shelter and thereby improve its appearance.

Other sites
Even the composting corner of the garden can be brightened up as the bars or grid of the composting container itself can provide an excellent climbing frame for plants.

Flowering, climbing plants, like sweet peas or nasturtiums, which will cover a container with their bright flowers in no time at all, will cheer up any dull corner of the garden. Planting soft fruit bushes, such as red/black/whitecurrants or gooseberries, or other low-growing shrubs, like lilac or forsythia, in front of a composting station will also aid the compost to ripen as maturing compost does not like to receive too much direct sunlight.

Position, planting and care

Your plants will thrive better if you create the best conditions for healthy growth right from the start. In order to do this you will need to know the individual requirements of the plants with respect to position and soil, when and how to plant them and how to care for them properly. If all of these conditions are met, your plants will flourish and be the envy of all who see them.

Shrubs that are ecologically beneficial
barberry (*Berberis vulgaris*)
broom (*Genista tinctoria*)
buckthorn (*Rhamnus catharticus*)*
cornelian cherry (*Cornus mas*)
elder (*Sambucus nigra* and *S. racemosa*)*
hedge maple (*Acer campestre*)
Frangula alnus
hawthorn (*Crataegus crusgalli*)
hazelnut (*Corylus avellana*)
holly (*Ilex aquifolium*)*
hornbeam (*Carpinus betulus*)
juniper (*Juniperus communis*)
privet (*Ligustrum vulgare*)*
Prunus mahaleb
sloe (*Prunus spinosa*)
snowy mespilus (*Amelanchier lamarckii*)
spindleberry (*Euonymus europaea*)*
whitethorn (*Crataegus monogyna*)
willow (*Salix*)

These bushes provide shelter and food for numerous species of birds and small creatures. (*toxic plants)

Planting

The right time to plant
The best time is in spring when the plants will have enough time to form proper roots and to grow well before the first frosts in late autumn.
Container plants or plants sold with a rootstock can be planted all year round but will require a great deal of care and attention. High temperatures during the daytime will inhibit growth.

Position
Light: Not all plants have the same requirements with respect to light. Generally, a distinction is made between:
● positions in full sunlight
● semi-shady positions, and
● shady positions.
Examples of climbing plants which require lots of light include roses and wisteria. However, most native European climbing plants normally grow wild in semi-shady positions on the fringes of woodland; for example hops. Ivy is a good shade provider in the wild.
Temperature: Sufficient warmth is essential to the survival of many plants. Sunny, and therefore warm, positions are ideal for frost-sensitive plants like woody espalier plants or large container plants. Flowering climbing plants will also thrive here. Evergreen climbing plants prefer positions with a more balanced temperature (even north-facing).
Soil: Depending on their requirements, individual plants will thrive in various different kinds of soil. Even if the soil has been improved (see p. 22), you should not try to grow plants that require a rich soil in a very poor one.
Water: Most climbing plants require a plentiful supply of water to help them to absorb the nutrients in the soil.

Planting in open soil
The work involved in planting and care is less involved if you plant directly into open soil as, here, climbing plants will find the kind of conditions that most closely resemble those of their natural habitat:
● They are growing directly in the soil, so they have plenty of space for their roots to grow.
● They will be supplied with plenty of rainwater.

On a patio

Depending on the site of the patio, you may have to provide protection from the wind in order to obtain a really sheltered position for Mediterranean plants or espalier fruit trees. As most patios are situated on the south side of the house, the plants planted or kept there are subject to intense sunlight and considerable differences in temperature during the course of the day. More watering by the gardener will therefore be needed than for plants planted in open soil (see p. 26).

The soil in beds along the sides of new patios is often mixed with builders' rubble and will have to be improved before you plant anything (see p. 22).

On a balcony

Balconies share many features of a patio but the amount of light received may be impaired by neighbouring balconies or shadows created by other nearby buildings. During the summer, balconies may turn into real heat traps for plants, as heat reflected from road surfaces or house walls may collect there. It is, therefore, particularly important to provide suitable shading and to water the plants adequately (see p. 26). What to watch out for when planting in balcony boxes is explained on page 24.

Virginia creeper will provide a protective covering for your house.

21

Planting beside walls

Dig a planting hole, lay a piece of filter fabric in it and fill the space between the hole and the wall with gravel. Mix dug out soil with improving substances. Insert the plant, lean the support stick against the wall and fill up the hole with soil.

Types of soil and how to improve them

As a rule, climbing plants demand fairly loose, nutrient-rich soil such as humus-rich garden soil. As most soils do not possess all the features of an ideal plant soil, they have to be improved with loosening or binding substances and should receive basic fertilization before planting commences (see p.28).

Sandy soils generally contain very little humus.

● Characteristics: A fine, crumbly structure, therefore very water-permeable and easy for roots to penetrate, but with a decreased capacity for storing nutrients.
● Improvement: Use organic fertilizers and binding substances like loam and organic compost.

Loamy soils often contain plenty of humus.

● Characteristics: If there is a high clay content, it may be difficult for roots to penetrate. A loamy soil should have a good capacity for retaining nutrients. If it dries out severely, large cracks may cause damage to roots.
● Improvement: Use sand for loosening and compost or stable manure as fertilizer to turn it into an ideal growing medium.

Chalky soils, depending on their situation, will naturally tend to contain a thin or thicker layer of humus.

● Characteristics: Usually lumpy or gravelly so very permeable for water and nutrients.
● Improvement: Use sand and compost for loosening, and stable manure and mineral fertilizers for fertilizing.

Peaty or marshy soils will have either a thin or thick layer of humus on top.

● Characteristics: As a rule, poor in nutrients, loose and easy for roots to penetrate when drained; not a good growing medium.
● Improvement: Add mineral fertilizers and lime.

Soil exchange: An exchange of soil is necessary if climbing plants are to be planted beside a wall where soil is often full of builders' rubble or is very compact (very difficult for roots to penetrate). In some cases, you may even have to remove flagstones, tiles or similar coverings beforehand. Unwanted material like chunks of concrete, stone chippings or coarse gravel, should be completely removed. The remaining soil should be improved with humus, fertilizer (mineral or organic, see. p. 27) and, depending on the type of soil, with loosening or binding substances.

Compost for plants in large containers and boxes

Plants which have to make do with small volumes of soil or compost must be supplied with compost that is adapted to their requirements.

Ripe garden compost is very rich in nutrients and very suitable for growing plants. It can be taken as waste matter from a kitchen garden or made from vegetable and plant kitchen scraps etc. in a compost heap in your own garden. You can buy special composting bins in the gardening trade. Suitable growing mediums are also sold as ready-to-use products in garden centres etc.

Standard compost, which is sold in bags, usually consists of loamy soil and peat. Often, loosening substances like polystyrene fragments and fertilizer are mixed in with it so that this compost can be used for planting without further preparation.

Peat consists of the dead parts of marginal plants. Due to its very fibrous structure, peat acts as a loosening agent in compost and soil. It absorbs and stores water well and is contained in many commercial composts. Despite this, environmentally aware gardeners are now recommended to avoid using peat as much as possible as producing it contributes to the destruction and loss of large areas of natural wetlands and moors.

Ordinary garden soil is rarely suitable for large containers. Depending on its consistency, soil-improving substances will probably have to be added to it.

Pruning

Climbing plants which can be bought in tree nurseries and are sold with roots but without soil around them, should be cut back immediately before planting. The above-ground shoots should be cut back by about one third of their length, and the roots by about 1-2 cm (½-¾ in).

Damaged roots or those that have obviously dried up should be cut back to where they look healthy. Thicker main roots (more than a finger wide) should be left.

Container plants should not have their roots cut back and the shoots should be pruned only sparingly as plants with a properly covered rootstock should not suffer shock from being replanted.

Shrubs and annual climbing plants that are almost exclusively obtainable as container plants should not be cut back before planting.

The correct way to plant

The way a plant is planted affects the way it will grow. It is, therefore, particularly important to observe a few basic rules when planting in a well-prepared position so that the plant is sure to thrive.

Planting in open soil

When preparing a planting hole, you should check, even before buying the plant, that the soil is loose, easy for roots to penetrate and not too sandy. A small "trial hole" of about two spades' depth can be dug to check this point. If the soil is too stony or contains too much clay, you can buy the necessary improving substances at the same time as the plant (see p. 22). Exchanging the soil later on, after planting, is both difficult and usually harmful to the plant.

NB: The size of the planting hole depends on the size of the rootstock which should have enough room in the hole to expand. As a general rule, be guided by the standard dimensions of 60 x 60 x 60 cm (24 x 24 x 24 in).

Method
● Dig the planting hole.
● When digging, make sure that the darker soil on top is not mixed with the lighter soil underneath; if possible, pile them up separately.
● The bottom of the planting hole should be loosened up with a spade, shovel or a pick, to a depth of at least 20 cm (8 in).
● Carefully remove the plant from its container, stand it in the planting hole and check the position.
● Take the plant out again and place some of the lighter undersoil, mixed with soil-improvement substances or compost (mixing ratio 1:1), in the hole so that, when placed in the hole, the neck of the root of the plant will be level with the top edge of the hole.
● If the plants have been bought with the rootstock tied in a covering such as sacking, make sure you loosen the cloth at the neck and remove any tight strings. The cloth should remain around the roots as it will decay in time.
● Now, shovel in the rest of the dark topsoil, mixed with controlled-release fertilizer (hoof and horn chips or mineral fertilizer, see p. 27), making sure that you follow the manufacturer's instructions. Place this around the plant and tread it down firmly.
● Use the remaining soil to create a shallow gulley around the plant for watering purposes.

Care after planting
● Water the plants well (about 5-10 litres/9-18 pt or more, depending on the size of the plant).
● Self-climbing plants should be trained towards the wall using the stick to which the young plant was tied when bought, in order to give the plant some hold (see p. 22).
● Remove the support sticks of plants with tendrils and winding plants and immediately tie the plant to the climbing aid which you have already installed.
● After watering, protect the planting area from drying out by mulching (using straw, grass cuttings or bark mulch). This will also prevent the growth of weeds.

Planting directly beside a wall
If the planting area is right beside a house or garage wall that would be damaged by moisture or water splashes, the wall should be given a coat of insulating paint. If this cannot be done, a layer of gravel, approximately 40 cm (16 in) wide (see p. 22), should be laid between the wall and the planting area.

Drainage in a large container

Place a 5-10 cm (2-4 in) thick layer of drainage material in the container. Lay filter fabric on top and draw it up to the inside edge of the container. Add the compost. Stand the plant in the container, shovel in compost between the pot and the rootstock and press down firmly. Water well.

Spindleberry.

Clematis hybrid.

Honeysuckle.

You will require: gravel (16 mm in diameter) and filtering fabric.

Method
● To protect the wall, dig a trench 30-40 cm (12-16 in) wide and 20 cm (8 in) deep along it.
● Dig out the actual planting area adjacent to it (approx. 60 cm/ 24 in wide and 60 cm/24 in deep). Then treat the dug out soil in the same way as when planting in open soil (see p. 23).
● Fill the shallow pit along the wall with gravel.
● Lay the filtering fabric between the layer of gravel and the planting area.
● Insert the plant and then fill up the planting area with soil.
NB: All work carried out outside the boundaries of your property will require permission from a local authority or neighbour.

Planting in large containers and boxes
When choosing the height of the container, consider the eventual height of the plant and the size of its rootstock. The plant will need enough space for its roots to spread out and should not be squeezed into its container.
NB: To give protection against freezing in winter, an insulating liner should be placed in the container before inserting the drainage layer (see p. 29).
Drainage: To prevent waterlogging or a blockage of the drainage holes, before planting, larger containers should first be equipped with a 5-10 cm (2-4 in) layer of gravel (of about 8-16 mm diameter) or with Hortag. Hortag is considerably lighter than gravel and is therefore ideal for large, heavy plant containers. Cover the

drainage holes with broken pieces of pot beforehand. Over the drainage layer spread a layer of fabric filter which should then be pulled up around the sides to the top edge of the container. This will prevent compost or soil being washed down the sides of the fabric and into the drainage layer.
Planting
● After planting, carefully water the plant but do not flood it.
● It is better to water several times sparingly on a daily basis.
● If the planting medium has sunk down a little after a few days, top up the container with extra compost and form a watering gulley (see p. 23).
● Do not fertilize plants bought in the gardening trade until about six weeks after planting, as they will already have been provided with controlled-release fertilizer.

Morning glory and ornamental gourd.

Russian vine.

Climbing rose.

Plants from other sources can have controlled-release fertilizer mixed in with their compost. Once you have done this, do not fertilize again for another four weeks.
Balcony boxes with summer flowers planted in them will not require a drainage layer as they are not very deep. They should, however, still have drainage holes which should be covered with fragments of broken pot.
● An ordinary balcony box that is only 12 cm (4¾ in) wide, 15 cm (6 in) deep will be too small for perennial climbing plants. They require containers with a capacity of at least 30-40 litres.
● Annual climbing plants, on the other hand, will manage in standard-size balcony boxes (see pp. 26 and 27) as long as they are given the right amount of water and fertilizer.

● Adequate protection from frost (see p. 29) will also be necessary for balcony boxes if the plants are expected to overwinter in them.

Planting annual climbing plants

Annuals that are pre-grown in pots or large containers often have a headstart with respect to growth but, having begun life in a greenhouse, are also often more sensitive than hardened, home-grown plants.
Sowing and raising: The seed of many climbing plants can be bought or collected and sown in pots (larger seeds) or seed trays. The seeding compost in the seed tray should be moistened slightly (use a spray bottle) and the seed tray should be covered with a transparent lid or cling film. Also cover pots with cling film. From

time to time, lift the film or lid for ventilation.
Pots or seed trays should be placed in a warm, light but not too bright spot; the seeds require a temperature of about 20°C (68°F) to germinate. During this time, keep the surface of the seeding compost slightly moist. The germinating seeds are usually too densely packed in a tray to develop fully. The tiny plantlets have to be thinned out to provide more space when two germ leaves are fully developed. The space between rows should be 10 cm (4 in) and the spaces between individual plants 5 cm (2 in) (see illustration, p. 26).
Sowing in open soil: You can obtain the seeds of many annual climbing plants in the gardening trade. These can be sown straight into open soil.

Particularly robust species, like runner beans, nasturtiums and convolvulous, are particularly suited to this method:

● Soak larger seeds in lukewarm water overnight to speed up germination.

● Make a 5 cm (2 in) deep drill in loose garden soil (for several plants growing beside each other) or a 5 cm (2 in) deep hole for each seed (check the instructions for depth on the packet).

● Lay the seeds in the hole (if there are several, ensure correct spacing which should be indicated on the packet, probably three to five seeds) and cover them with soil.

● The seeds will germinate sooner if you lay a piece of plastic sheeting over the planting area, weighted down with stones around the edges. Once the seedlings appear, the sheet can be removed or raised on wooden or wire sticks so that the plants have room to grow. It is advisable not to plant seeds before the last cold snap towards the middle of the last month of spring as the young plants will not cope with frost.

Planting in open soil: Annual climbing plants have very special soil requirements because of their rapid growth and they also require a good supply of nutrients. The hole should be dug as described on page 23. However, a hole with a depth of 30 cm (12 in) will be sufficient.

Planting in large containers and boxes: If your home-grown or bought annual climbing plants are to be planted in a large container or balcony box, proceed as for planting in large containers (see p. 24).

Sowing seed in a seed tray and pricking out
Sow the seed evenly, using a folded piece of paper. Cover the seed tray with cling film. Loosen the seedlings from the growing medium with the thin end of a pricking out tool. Make a hole with the thick end of the pricking out tool and plant the seedling deep enough for the first leaves to lie on the surface of the growing medium. Press down lightly.

Care

If you know what a plant's requirements are, you can ensure that it has the best possible care. Every plant has to be supplied with an adequate amount of water and nutrients. There are also other measures of care to attend to for climbing plants, such as tying up shoots, the occasional pruning and, if necessary, providing protection against cold and frost. Plants which are not growing in open soil, but are planted in large containers or boxes, are particularly dependent on regular and sometimes intensive care.

Watering

Water is essential for all plants. The amount of water that plants lose daily through evaporation from their leaves depends on the temperature on that day, the humidity and the amount of direct sunlight. The following rule applies: the cooler the day and the higher the humidity, the less water the plants will require.
NB: Do not water plants during midday or in intense direct sunlight.
Plants in open soil need not be watered quite as often as plants in

large containers or boxes on account of their widely spreading root systems.

● It is important that you water thoroughly so that even the deepest roots are adequately supplied with moisture.

● Young or recently planted plants need more frequent watering. For the rest, it will be sufficient to water every eight to ten days during the main growth period (from the second month of spring to the second month of autumn).

● Annual climbing plants that are situated in a sunny position should be watered more often.

● During the winter, water evergreen climbing plants like ivy only occasionally and only on frost-free days.

Plants in large containers and boxes, which contain relatively little compost, will use up water rapidly.

How often you water will depend on the individual requirements of plants, the size of the planting container and on the weather. The basic rule is:

● Plants in pots should be watered more often than those growing in open soil.

● Large, vigorously growing plants in pots require more frequent watering as the supply of water in the rootstock will be used up more quickly.

● On hot summer days, water plants growing on a patio or balcony twice daily, preferably in the morning and evening.

● Consider what type of containers the plants are in: water will not evaporate quite so quickly from plastic containers as from clay containers.

● You can usually tell by looking at the leaves whether plants need water: if they are drooping or the leaves are rolled up, they are in desperate need of water.

The "finger test" will determine whether a plant is thirsty. Push a finger about 1 cm deep into the top of the compost. If it feels damp you will not need to water that day; if it feels dry, water well.

Rainwater is still to be recommended for watering, despite the increase in pollution, and is still better for plants than hard, lime-rich mains water. Mains water should be left to stand for a few days before using it.

Watering during holidays: Watering large container or balcony plants can be a problem if you are to be away from home for any length of time. Irrigation systems are on sale in the gardening trade but you should always test these thoroughly before you go away to make sure that they work properly. If you are going away for a brief holiday, you should be able to manage by using plant containers with inbuilt water reservoirs (see p. 14). The most reliable "system", however, is still a friend or accommodating neighbour who will follow your written instructions!

My tip: Watering balcony boxes that are attached to the outside of a balcony railing may cause inconvenience to neighbours with balconies under yours. If you do not have very tolerant neighbours downstairs, it is probably better to hang the boxes on the inside of the railing.

Fertilizing

Plants require certain nutrients for growth and well-being. Particularly during the vegetative period, while the plant is growing and flowering, it should be provided with sufficient nutrients. Nutrients that are lacking in the soil or compost must be replaced and this is done by fertilizing. Some species like a lot of fertilizer, such as runner beans or ornamental gourds, while other, less demanding, plants, such as wild forms of clematis and ivy, manage on very little.

The frequency of fertilizing during the growth period depends on the individual plant species and is described in the instructions for care (see pp. 39-59).

Types of fertilizer: Fertilizers are available in solid, dried or liquid form.

● Liquid fertilizers do not need to be dissolved in water first and are particularly suitable for plants in large containers or on balconies.

● Solid fertilizers are mixed with the soil or compost and will gradually release nutrients to the plant as these nutrients must first be broken down through the action of water.

The nutrient composition of fertilizers: In addition to the three main nutrients of nitrogen (N), phosphorus (P) and potassium (K), plants also need lesser quantities of trace elements like magnesium, iron, sulphur, copper, boron and manganese.

● Nitrogen supports the upward growth of plants and the development of leaves. Nitrogen deficiency is recognizable by yellow leaves and stunted growth.

● Phosphorus is necessary for the formation of roots, flowers and fruit.

● Potassium builds up the plant's resistance to disease and pests.

Compound fertilizer (mineral and inorganic fertilizer) contains all of the main nutrients. However, the nutrient composition is not the same for all fertilizers. The proportions of main nutrients in any fertilizer are always expressed as the abbreviation N P K, and given as a ratio in that order on the outside of the packaging. Thus, 7:7:7 means equal proportions of nitrogen, phosphorus and potassium are included, each nutrient comprising 7 per cent of the total content. **NB:** 20 g mineral fertilizer per square metre (40 sq in) is enough.

Types of fertilizer

● Mineral fertilizers or inorganic fertilizers contain nutrients in the form of soluble salts. When given to the plant as granules, they are dissolved by water and washed down among the roots. Controlled-release fertilizer contains nutrients in the form of small beads which release the nutrients very gradually over a period of time aided by the action of moisture.

● Organic (or biological) fertilizers consist of animal products like ground hoof and horn, horn chips, dried blood, animal dung or plant extracts. This type of fertilizer often provides only one nutrient: animal manure and horn chips, for example, provide nitrogen; bonemeal provides phosphorus. Organic fertilizers are generally not compound fertilizers and it takes a relatively long time for the nutrients to become effective.

An attractive visual screen – a wire fence covered with ivy and Virginia creeper.

How often to fertilize
Plants growing in open soil need not be fertilized quite so often as plants in large containers or boxes, as they can draw on a natural reservoir of soil nutrients. Large container plants and balcony plants have to be supplied with fertilizer on a regular basis in order to balance the disadvantages created by their positions.
● One or two doses of fertilizer will be sufficient for perennial climbing plants during the vegetation period.

● Annual climbing plants that are growing in open soil require regular fertilizing at intervals of about four to six weeks over their short growing period.
● A weekly dose of fertilizer is recommended for plants in smaller containers or pots; fortnightly fertilizing will be sufficient for larger containers (from 30-40 cm/12-16 in high).
● Large container plants should not be fertilized after the end of summer so that they can prepare themselves for winter.

As a basic fertilizer for woody plants: mix the main nutrients NPK (ratio 10:10:15) with the planting medium if you are not using compost that already contains fertilizer.
Plants sold with a rootstock, or container plants, will welcome a starter boost from an organic fertilizer. Plants in pots should be fertilized again about six to eight weeks after planting. Plants in open soil should be fertilized about two to three months after planting.

The right way to fertilize
● Only provide fertilizer if the plant is able to absorb nutrients; that is, during the growth phase from spring to autumn.
● Always read the manufacturer's instructions regarding dosage.
● Never strew the fertilizer on dry soil or compost as the roots would soon suffer burns from such a high concentration of nutrients.
● Always mix controlled-release fertilizer with the soil or compost.

Mistakes in fertilizing
● Signs of a lack of fertilizer: Meagre growth, lack of flowers, light-coloured or discoloured leaves. An immediate dose of compound fertilizer will help, preferably in liquid form.
● Signs of an excess of fertilizer: Brown spots on leaves or burned edges to leaves, unnaturally long shoots, very large, limp leaves. Remedy: In the case of potted plants, thoroughly drench the area of the roots in running water. This is best done in a bath. Do not water the plant again for about three days. In the case of plants growing in open soil, all you can do is water very thoroughly.

Tying up
It is sometimes necessary to tie parts of climbing plants to a support as, occasionally, the plants will not manage to find the support provided on their own or will simply send their shoots out in another direction.
Even self-climbers like ivy or Virginia creeper are grateful for initial help in training them towards a wall or fence.
Ramblers, like climbing roses, will need to have their new shoots tied up regularly.
In the case of espalier fruit, tying up is very important as it serves to anchor the new growth, determines the direction in which the plant will continue to grow and stimulates fruit production (see tying up espaliers, p. 32).

Plant-friendly tying materials include garden twine, hemp string or rope and rubberized wire.
NB: When tying up plants, give consideration to the potential thickness of the shoots; the tie should not be too tight around the shoot as this will interfere with transportation of water and nutrients and the outer skin of the shoot may be rubbed raw or damaged. The best way to proceed is to make a loose loop around the shoot, tie a second loop around the support stick etc. and then finish off this loop with a knot, making a figure of eight.

Pruning
Generally speaking, climbing plants do not require much pruning but will cope with it quite well as a rule. Otherwise, only frost-damaged shoots need cutting back to green, healthy wood in the spring.

Winter protection
By late autumn sufficient winter protection should be provided against severe frost. The first step towards this is made by choosing hardy plants in the first place and then planting them in the right position, for example somewhere sheltered.
Frost protection in open soil: It is mainly young plants that are at risk here but roses and warmth-loving climbing plants will also be very grateful for some form of protection when the temperature drops below zero.
How to protect your plants
● Heaping up soil around the stem, to a height of 20-30 cm (8-12 in), and covering this with brushwood, straw or conifer branches (also to a height of 20-30 cm/8-12 in) will protect the plants from freezing to death.
● Climbing roses or more sensitive climbing plants like wisteria can also be wrapped in bundles of straw or brushwood along the length of their longer shoots.
● In the case of evergreen climbing plants, frost damage can be avoided by watering the plants thoroughly during the autumn and also on frost-free days in winter. Lack of water will increase susceptibility to frost damage.
Frost protection for plant containers: If you wish to overwinter perennial climbers in large containers on a balcony or patio, you will have to provide adequate insulation of the containers against frost.

Method
● Before planting or inserting a drainage layer (see p. 24), line the inside walls of the container with 5-10 mm thick polystyrene sheeting. The drainage layer will protect the floor of the container against freezing.
● If the container is round, draw the filter fabric up to about 5 cm (2 in) below the upper edge of the container and insert a 1-2 cm (½-¾ in) layer of coarse sand or grit between the wall of the container and the layer of fabric.
● Always choose containers that are frost-proof for overwintering outside (see p. 13).
● Cover up plants in large containers with brushwood or straw.
NB: Large container plants, for example oleander or fuchsia, cannot be overwintered outside and will require particular conditions in their winter quarters so it is important to find out about any such requirements before you purchase sensitive plants in order to avoid disappointment later.

Fruit espaliers

One of the reasons why espaliers are so popular is their dual blessing of attractive foliage and a harvest of fruit. Espalier fruit trees bear enchanting blossoms and you can also fulfil your ambition of picking fresh pears, apples, peaches or apricots straight from your own house wall. Some most decorative forms of espalier can be created, even by novice gardeners.

Points to note about fruit espaliers

The difference between espalier fruit trees and fruit trees grown in open soil is that an artificial shape of growth is produced by tying up and judicious pruning. This makes it possible to produce tasty, fully ripened fruit in a small space, for example on a house or garage wall.

Growing aids for espaliers

There are various different possibilities for growing espalier fruit on a wall. All methods involve directing the shoots into the desired shape by fixing them to a growing aid. The following are suitable growing aids:
● Wooden frames made of battens or sticks (see p. 12).
● Horizontally and/or vertically stretched wires (depending on the shape of the espalier) which have to be fixed to the wall with the aid of dowelled wall hooks.
● Horizontal wires drawn tautly between two wooden posts which are about 8-10 cm (3-4 in) thick. At each end of the planting area you should drive the wooden posts into the soil slightly at an angle and at least 70 cm (28 in) deep. Depending on the height of the espalier, the posts may protrude up to 2 m (7 ft) above the soil.

NB: All growing aids should be a minimum distance of 10-30 cm (4-12 in) from the house wall (see p. 11) and should be erected and fixed to the wall before planting.

Shapes of espaliers

These fruit-bearing woody plants can be used to enhance a facade in many different forms. Both stems and branches can be trained into geometric shapes. The average height of growth of individual plants is important in determining the final shape of the espalier; vigorously growing varieties, such as pears, for example, can be trained to cover an entire house wall with greenery.

The most commonly seen espalier shapes are:
● A cordon which is the simplest espalier shape. It consists of a vertical stem or trunk without any lateral branches and is, therefore, very suitable for narrow spaces, for example between a door and a window. The distance between two such trees should be no less than 50-60 cm (20-24 in); only plant varieties with similar speeds of growth beside each other.

● A U-shape, which forms a "double" cordon without a continuous main shoot. The space between individual branches should be 60-80 cm (24-32 in) (see p. 31).
● A palmette with a broad fan shape and much branching; this is particularly suitable for vigorously growing varieties in larger areas (see p. 31).
● A high espalier, for which a long, vertical stem is first grown and lateral branching is allowed to begin at a certain height (for example around windows on the ground floor). This shape may grow right up to the gable of a house and is often used for vigorously growing pear trees.

NB: When choosing the shape of an espalier you must always consider the speed and final extent of growth of the fruit tree.

Suitable fruit species

Species suitable for planting as espaliers are: apples, pears, peaches, apricots and grapevines. Growing fruit against a house wall in this way brings the benefit of extra warmth, so that, even in regions with a rougher climate, gardeners can still grow their own fruit.

Information about the positioning and care of the espalier fruit varieties mentioned here can be found on pages 56-9.

Planting and care of espalier fruit trees

Fruit grown on espaliers requires more intensive care than that given to perennial climbing plants in open soil: in addition to fertilizing and watering, careful pruning and regular tying up are essential if you want to obtain a worthwhile harvest.

The best position

Fruit growing requires special climatic conditions. Before you decide on the varieties you intend to buy, do make a realistic assessment of your normal climate and temperature. If you give this information to the nursery from which you are ordering plants, their expert staff will be able to advise you if your choice is unsuitable and suggest alternatives.

A house wall that you intend to use for growing espalier fruit should meet the following requirements:

● The wall should be situated in a sheltered position, as draughts will prevent the plant from benefiting from accumulated warmth.

● It should be well ventilated; that is, there must be adequate space between the wall and the espalier.

● The more sun that reaches the wall, the more demanding the types of fruit you can try to grow on it.

The best side of the house for establishing an espalier is the south-facing one. Even in unfavourable regions (high altitude, areas affected by late frosts), you can often plant

particularly warmth-loving varieties of fruit, such as peaches, apricots or late-ripening varieties, against a south-facing wall.

Planting them too close together may cause the plants to be harmed by temperatures that become too high. Insufficient ventilation between the wall and the espalier will encourage fungal infection, such as mildew, in many fruit varieties (see p. 35).

NB: Many house walls are not adequately protected against the water splashes and rising damp that may penetrate from the adjoining planting area (see planting against walls, p. 23).

The right soil

In many cases, the soil immediately in front of a wall is not suitable for growing espalier fruit unless it has been adequately prepared beforehand. Large items such as tiles, flagstones, asphalt, etc. will have to be removed before planting and the soil underneath must be replaced with suitable soil (see p. 22). The length of the planting hole will depend on the desired width of the espalier, but the minimum depth and width of the hole should not be less than 1 m (40 in).

Palmette
This shape can be created with four, six or more arms. Never choose an uneven number of branches for this palmette as the tree will look unbalanced.

As a rule, *fruit trees* prefer a warm, permeable, crumbly, moist soil. In addition to these characteristics, the right nutrient content is also of great importance (see p. 32). Pure humus soils or garden soils are usually deficient in minerals. By mixing in the right fertilizers, both the nutrient content and the mineral content can be improved (see soil improvement, p. 22).

NB: Information on the soil requirements of popular espalier fruits can be found on pages 56-9.

The correct way to plant

Espalier fruit should be pruned immediately before planting, when all branches should be cut back by about one third of their length. Before planting, also cut back the fine roots slightly, thereby encouraging renewed root formation. When planting espalier fruit, you should note the following points:

● Soak the rootstock of the young tree in a bucket before planting.

A U-shaped fruit espalier

Stand the espalier tree in the planting hole and mark the positions for the wall hooks on the wall. Take the tree out, fix the hooks to the wall and draw wires between them (corresponding to the shape of the espalier). Insert the tree in the hole. Tie the little tree to the growing aid. Check the ties from time to time to make sure they are not too tight or loose.

Planting trees

Stand the young tree in the prepared planting hole. Fill the hole with soil and tie the tree to a wooden support stick. The grafting point should end up about a hand span above the soil. Make a gulley for watering and water the young tree well.

● Dig out the planting hole (see planting in open soil, p. 23), loosen the soil well and fill the hole again, to about two thirds, with soil.

● Drive a wooden stake into the soil as a support for the young tree (diameter 8-10 cm/3-5 in).

● Stand the young tree in the planting hole, shovel in the rest of the soil and tread it down firmly all around the tree.

● The grafting point (recognizable as a lump at the lower end of the stem) must remain above the soil or roots will start forming from it that will grow into unwelcome wild shoots which will draw energy and nutrients from the grafted fruit variety.

● Tie the young tree to the support stake using a figure of eight loop made of coconut fibre or hemp twine, and then nail the tie to the post so it cannot slip down.

● Leave a gulley for watering around the tree (see p. 23) and water well.

● Tie the shoots of the young tree to the growing aid in the desired shape.

Fertilizing espalier fruit

A soil containing a balanced ratio of organic and mineral nutrients is an important precondition for the healthy development of an espalier tree.

Nitrogen will encourage the roots to develop and shoots to grow. If too much nitrogen is supplied, however, the trees will become susceptible to disease and the fruit will rapidly decay.

Phosphorus encourages the formation of fruit and the ripening process and ensures good flavour.

Potassium strengthens the plant and is important for good wood and fruit formation.

How often to fertilize

Fertilizer mixed in with the soil at the time of planting will last for the first year. Well-established espalier fruit trees should be fertilized two or three times a year; the best times are in the spring when the plant starts growing again and after the harvest, around the time when the wood ripens, to encourage resistance against frost.

Espalier fruit trees like fertilizer such as:

● well-rotted manure
● compound fertilizer (see p. 27)
● garden compost that is

mixed with organic fertilizer.

● In addition to compost or compound fertilizer, you should also give the plants fermented plant brews in the spring and autumn. A combination of fermented nettle and borage brew (see p. 37) acts as both a fertilizer and an effective plant protection agent.

NB: Avoid unripened, fresh manure as this can burn the roots.

Water sparingly, but regularly

The area around the plant should be kept fairly moist, although fruit trees do not like "wet feet". Waterlogging in the area of the roots may cause them to die off.

NB: When fruit espaliers are grown against very sunny walls, you may have to water twice on very hot summer days.

A short-term period of dryness will not damage the espalier fruit unduly.

Tying espaliers

Tying performs several functions in the case of espalier fruit. It serves to:

● fasten the shoots to the climbing aid
● train the shoots in the desired direction of growth
● encourage fruit formation.

Tying horizontally encourages the food made by the leaves through photosynthesis to be stored in the flower buds and thereby aids fruit formation. (Vertical shoots tend to produce leaves rather than buds.)

When trained horizontally, espaliers require less pruning as fewer vertical shoots are formed. The general rule is to cut less and tie up more.

How to train for horizontal growth:

Humidity makes wood more

flexible, so the best time to tie up branches is in the morning or evening.

● Persuading the first branches of a young fruit tree to grow in a horizontal plane without breaking is made easier by hanging small metal tags or clay pots on them (tied on with string around the middle of the branch). The branches will gradually be pulled down by the weight.

● Suitable materials for tying are garden twine, hemp string, parcel string, or even coconut fibre rope for larger branches.

● The branches should be tied to the growing frame by means of loose figure of eight loops.

NB: The branches should not end up drooping downwards but should be more or less horizontal.

Grafting fruit varieties

As a rule, espalier fruit trees are grafted on to the stock of another fruit tree, sometimes even on to another fruit species. Grafting makes it possible to combine very different qualities of two varieties of fruit, for example combining a good yield with hardiness to frost or resistance against fungal infections and a prolific formation of fruit or larger fruit. The grafting point is generally thicker than the rest of the stem on account of the extra tissue that has formed at the point of cutting. It may be either directly above the neck of the root or (in the case of quince or cherry) on the upper end of the stem just below the branches. The grafting of fruit varieties is carried out in specialist nurseries. If you wish to know more about it, you can obtain information from your local gardening society or plant nursery.

A vigorous stock grown from a seedling has the following advantages: it is robust and undemanding; it is suitable for positions where the soil quality is not very good or the climate is rough; it is recommended for wall espaliers, especially high ones.

A less vigorously growing stock is better suited to smaller areas, for example between windows.

NB: Before buying any fruit tree for training into an espalier, you should find out from the nursery whether the stock and the espalier shape you are planning to grow are suited to each other.

Pruning espalier fruit trees

It is not possible within the limited scope of this volume to cover the various methods of pruning in great detail and you would be well advised to consult other, specialist literature on this subject (enquire at your local library or garden centre). I have, however, included a few basic pieces of information.

When to prune

There are many different opinions on this matter. However, the following basic rule can be applied: *The main time for pruning is in early spring* when the tree has hardly any foliage. At any other time severe pruning carries a risk

Thinning out cut
The old and infertile shoots are removed (see marked cutting points, left) so that light and air will be able to penetrate the crown.

of the tree being badly debilitated or even killed through loss of sap. Spring pruning can include removing branches and shoot tips that died during the winter. Pruning is also simpler at this time as the fruit and leaf buds are better formed and therefore more easily seen.

General rule: Fruit buds are usually larger than leaf buds. If you cannot distinguish them, ask an expert to identify them for you the first time or else simply decide for yourself and wait to see what appears when the bud opens.

Autumn is also a time for pruning espalier fruit trees. Do not do this too early, however, as the trees will still be producing too much sap and the wood will not have matured. Ripe wood will survive the winter better. (A sign of ripened wood is when the leaves start to discolour and finally fall off.)

My tip: Prune your trees again after the harvest is over as this will strengthen them.

For pruning you will need a strong pair of secateurs, a wound-sealing substance, a small saw and a sharp, preferably slightly curved, knife.

NB: The secateurs should be your main tool when pruning. If you have to start sawing away, it usually indicates that you have previously neglected a few necessary duties. Remember that it is better to prune more often and cut away less each time.

Tips on pruning

● Mark the branches with coloured wax crayon before cutting as this will help you to take off the right branches.

● Cut the branches off straight, using secateurs. Any ragged or frayed cuts should be cut cleanly with a sharp knife afterwards.

● Cut surfaces that are larger than a fifty pence coin should be treated with a wound-sealing substance to encourage growth of new tissue and to prevent the secretion of sap.

● If a large branch is cut right beside the main stem or taken from the crown, make sure that no stumps remain to create a risk of invasion by fungal infection.

Training cut

This can be used to give your espalier tree the right shape of crown during its first year, as this will be determined by the main shoots. As the espalier is basically a flattened shape, you should allow only lateral branches to remain as main shoots in order to create the correct shape; all other shoots should be cut back to the stem and the cut surfaces treated with a wound sealant. Weaker shoots and those that tend to the vertical should be removed during the training cut. Only the main shoots which will produce the branches that will bear the fruit should be left.

A thinning-out cut

A thinning-out cut should be undertaken in fruit trees for the following reasons:
● To provide the crown with sufficient light and ventilation.
● To maintain a balance between growth and fertility in the tree (see illustration, p. 33).

Pests and diseases

Plants die more often as a result of poor care than from diseases or attack by pests. Correct care is the best preventive measure against diseases and pests. When treating sick plants, avoid the thoughtless use of toxic spray in your garden. Very often biological plant protection agents will do the job and they are also kinder towards both plants and the environment.

Damage through the wrong kind of care

This can occur in all plants that are not cared for properly.

Waterlogging

Symptoms: Limp, faded shoots and leaves, often yellow discoloration. Damp soil or compost in large containers. Root tips are brown to black, decayed on the inside (check by pinching the root; healthy roots are light-coloured inside).
Cause: Too much watering or too often; absent or blocked drainage holes; no drainage; impermeable growth medium.
Prevention: Water carefully, provide an adequate number of drainage holes and a good drainage layer as well as loose, permeable compost or soil (mix in sand or grit).
Remedy: None.

Drying out

Symptoms: drooping, yellow leaves that dry up at the edges and roll up. Flowers fade and drop off prematurely. The roots turn brown.
Cause: Not enough water on hot or very windy days; a position that is too hot and sunny.
Prevention: Water more frequently during hot periods. Mix substances that store water with the soil or compost (for example, loamy soil or humus).
Remedy: Stand the rootstock in a container of lukewarm water for several hours. If damage is severe, nothing will help.

Nutrient deficiency

Symptoms: Nitrogen deficiency: pale leaves; meagre growth. *Phosphorus deficiency*: bluish-violet leaves. *Potassium deficiency*: weak shoots; brown leaf edges that roll up later on. *Magnesium deficiency:* leaves are yellow to brown with clearly marked leaf veins. *Iron deficiency* (chlorosis): leaves are yellow, leaf veins conspicuous.
Causes: The compost or soil contains too much lime (this prevents adequate absorption of nutrients); soil or compost is too compact or hard; not enough fertilizer.

Prevention: Loosen the soil once a month using a rake; water with rainwater; proper fertilizing.
Remedy: Provide the missing minerals. Remove the top layer of soil and replace it with a new layer containing mineral fertilizer.

Clematis wilt
Symptoms: Sudden death of healthy shoots.
Infested plants: Clematis hybrids; wild species are not so susceptible.
Prevention: Ensure adequate moisture during the growth period.
Remedy: None known at present.

Fungal diseases

Black spot
Symptoms: Small, blackish, round spots on leaves which die off after a while.
Infested plants: Often roses.
Prevention: Remove damaged leaves. Spray with mare's tail brew (see p. 37), repeat at intervals of several days.
Remedy: Spray, preferably with a biological preparation, repeat after a fortnight.

Pear rust
Symptoms: Orange-yellow spots (like rust spots) on leaves.
Infested plants: Pear trees.
Prevention: Ornamental juniper is an intermediate host for the fungus, so avoid ornamental juniper trees in gardens where pear trees are grown.
Remedy: Spray the pear trees, preferably with a biological preparation, repeat in 14 days.

Powdery mildew
Symptoms: a flour-like, white film on leaves and young parts of plants. Powdery mildew will also occur in dry weather.

This pear espalier has been growing here for many years.

Infested plants: Fruit trees, grapevines, roses, cucumbers. Powdery mildew will only be transmitted between plants of the same species.
Prevention: Ensure a well-ventilated position; spray several times with mare's tail brew (see p. 37) at intervals of a few days.
Remedy: Spray with preparations containing dinocap (see p. 37).

Downy mildew

Symptoms: whitish-yellow fungus spots on uppersides of leaves; a white fungus film on undersides of leaves. Occurs mainly in wet summers.
Infested plants: Roses, grapevine.
Prevention: A well-ventilated position. Spray with mare's tail brew at intervals of six weeks.
Remedy: Spray, preferably with a biological preparation (ask at your garden centre), repeat again after 10-14 days.

Trumpet vine is a fast-growing climbing plant.

Pests

Aphids

Symptoms: Black or green aphids on shoots and buds. Damage caused through sucking sap is visible on leaves, stalks and branches and can cause them to wilt and die. Rolled-up leaves. Infested plants: Roses, fruit trees, annual climbing plants, honeysuckle.
Prevention: Ensure a balanced nutrient supply as overfertilized plants are particularly susceptible to infestation by aphids. Fermented or fresh nettle brew (see p. 37) will strenthen the plant's resistance.
Control: Spray with tansy brew (see p. 37), repeat every few days; spray with agents containing pyrethrum (see p. 37).

Spider mites

Symptoms: The plants look limp, the leaves dry up and drop off. Small white spots on the leaves, gossamer-fine webs underneath.
Infested plants: Nasturtiums, honeysuckle, clematis hybrids, climbing roses, grapevine.
Prevention: Spray with nettle and mare's tail brew (see p. 37).
Control: Spray with an agent containing pyrethrum.

Codling moth and sawfly larvae (in apples)

Symptoms: To begin with, tiny eggs on the fruit, later holes in the fruit flesh and core; red-brown excrement at the entrances.
Infested plants: Apple trees.
Prevention: Remove all windfalls. Spray with tansy brew.
Control: Employ agents containing pyrethrum.

Scale insects

Symptoms: Light to dark brown scales stuck firmly to leaf undersides and leaf stalks. Damage caused by the sucking of sap from branches and stems.
Infested plants: Fruit trees, roses.
Prevention: Spray with tar-oil winter wash or tansy brew, repeating in several days.
Control: Brush down stems; spray with tar-oil.

Biological plant protection

Plant brews can be sprayed as a preventive and to protect against pests and fungal infections. Fermented plant brews are used as additional fertilizer to mineral and organic fertilizers, to strengthen and fortify plants.

Passion flower is a spendid flowering climber.

soil-balancing effect.

Fermented borage or comfrey brew contains large amounts of nitrogen and potassium. It is good for vigorously growing plants with lots of flowers.

Biological plant protection agents

Several such preparations can be bought in the gardening trade. They consist of herbal extracts, algae additives or pure chemical elements like sulphur or boron. The substances contained in these preparations can be present singly or mixed together. They are used mainly as brews for spraying.

Always follow the manufacturer's instructions when using them as some biological plant protection agents, for example pyrethrum, are toxic.

Pyrethrum agents contain pyrethrum which is obtained from a species of chrysanthemum. It is used to control aphids and mildew. It is not dangerous to bees.

Sulphur and dinocap preparations are used to control fungal infections.

Other herbal extracts, usually combined with sulphur or dinocap, can be used for controlling pear rust, mildew and scale insects.

NB: Never spray plant extracts in bright sunshine as they may cause the leaves to burn. Preferably spray under a cloudy sky, in mornings or evenings.

Warning: Children and domestic pets should be kept away when any such products are being sprayed.

Plant brews

Preparation: 1 kg (2¼ lb) fresh, coarsely chopped leaves or 200 g (7 oz) dried leaves in 10 litres (17¾ pt) cold water. Leave to soak for 24 hours, then boil for 30 minutes. Allow to cool, remove scum and use up quickly. Dilute the brew with water in the ratio of 1:2. This method can be used to prepare the following protective and fortifying brews:

Nettle brew has a strengthening and fortifying effect and is good for controlling aphids.

Tansy brew for controlling all kinds of insects (aphids, insect and moth larvae), leaf spot disease and mildew.

Mare's tail brew for controlling spider mites and mildew.

Fern brew (made from *Dryopteris*), undiluted: use as a prevention against scale insects.

Fermented herbal brews

Preparation: 1 kg (2¼ lb) fresh, coarsely chopped leaves or 200 g (7 oz) dried leaves in 10 litres (17¾ pt) cold water (preferably water that has been left to stand or, better still, rainwater). Leave the brew to stand in the sun (in a wooden or plastic container, never in a metal container). Fermentation will begin after two or three days. Stir thoroughly once daily. A fairly bad smell will be produced. The fermented brew will be ready to use after two or three weeks. Remove the scum, dilute the fermented brew with nine parts water and water the plants. This recipe can be used to prepare the following fermented plant brews:

Fermented nettle brew promotes resistance to disease, contains nitrogen and has a

Popular climbing plants and espalier fruit trees

The following pages present a selection of profusely flowering, easy-to-care-for climbing plants and varieties of espalier fruit, with photographs, descriptions and special notes on the correct care of each plant.

Glossary of keywords

The first name is the common name, which is followed by the botanical name (genus and species). The introduction gives details of the plant's climbing technique, its appearance, shape of growth and any individual characteristics.
Origin: An important clue to the correct care of the plant.
Flower/fruit: The main flowering time as well as details of flowers and the formation of fruit.
Position: Information on requirements in respect of temperature, wind, amount of sunlight and the right side of the house.
Soil: Advice on soil consistency in the open and for compost in containers.
Water: Tips on proper watering.
Fertilizing: Information on how often to fertilize and what to use.
Further care: Special tips on care and details on climbing aids (if necessary).

A pergola with clematis
Pergolas covered in greenery create a tranquil atmosphere.

Diseases/pests: Only given if the plant is particularly susceptible to certain diseases or pests (see also p. 34).
Overwintering: Only for plants that can be grown in a large container (see also p. 29).
Use: Only given if the plant is particularly suited to a certain manner of climbing/covering.
My tip: Extra tried and tested tips on care.

Key to symbols

 Position for the plant: south-facing, sunny.

 Position for the plant: west- and/or east-facing, semi-shady.

 Position for the plant: north-facing side, shady.

 This plant is also suitable for a large container.

 This plant is toxic.

List of plants

Annual climbing plants
Annual plants can be bought in the form of seeds for sowing at home or in pots (seedlings, young plants).

black-eyed Susan
(*Thunbergia alata*) 40
cathedral bell
(*Cobaea scandens*) 40
convolvulous
(*Convolvulous sepium*) 43
cucumber (*Cucumis sativus*) 42
morning glory (*Ipomoea tricolor*) 43
nasturtium (*Tropaeolum*) 41
ornamental gourd
(*Cucurbita pepo var. ovifera*) 42
runner bean
(*Phaseolus coccineus*) 41
sweet pea (*Lathyrus odoratus*) 44

Perennial climbing plants
Perennial plants can be bought pre-grown in the gardening trade.

clematis (*Clematis*) 54
Dutchman's pipe (*Aristolochia macrophylla*) 45
grapevine (*Vitis vinifera*) 51
honeysuckle (*Lonicera*) 45
hop (*Humulus lupulus*) 53
ivy (*Hedera helix*) 48
kiwi fruit (*Actinidia chinensis*) 52
roses (*Rosa*) 46
Russian vine (*Polygonum baldschaunica*) 52
spindleberry (*Euonymus fortunei*) 49
Virginia creeper
(*Parthenocissus*) 50
winter jasmine (*Jasminum nudiflorum*) 53
wisteria (*Wisteria sinensis*) 49

Espalier fruit tree species
Espalier fruit trees can be bought as young trees in tree nurseries

apple (*Malus domestica*) 59
apricot (*Prunus armeniaca*) 58
peach (*Prunus persica*) 57
pear (*Pyrus communis*) 56

Black-eyed Susan is ideal for balcony boxes.

Cathedral bell is a tireless bloomer.

Black-eyed Susan
Thunbergia alata

This annual winding plant, with heart-shaped, long-stalked, dark green leaves, will grow up to 2 m (7 ft) tall. It is a pretty, delicate summer-flowering plant.

Origin: South-east Africa, Madagascar.

Flower/fruit: Mid-summer to mid-autumn, funnel-shaped, yellow to orange single flowers with a dark centre, 5 cm (2 in) across. Fruit: Pea-sized, winged capsule with four seeds.

Position: Warm, sunny and sheltered from wind, south-facing.

Soil: Rich in nutrients and humus, standard compost in large container, loose growing medium.

Water: Water regularly but avoid waterlogging.

Fertilizing: In a large container and in open soil, every two weeks with liquid fertilizer; nettle brew also suitable.

Further care: Use a string or stick as a climbing aid. Tie the shoots to begin with. Pinching out shoot tips once will encourage the plant to branch out. Spacing of plants 60-80 cm (24-32 in).

Cathedral bell, cup and saucer vine
Cobaea scandens

This graceful annual grows up to 4 m (13 ft) tall. Its leaves are feathered and reddish when shooting. The leaf ends have been adapted into tendrils.

Origin: Mexico.

Flower/fruit: Flowers from mid-summer to the first frost. Bell-like flower, first whitish-green, later violet. White, red and blue varieties exist. Fruit: 5-7 cm (2-2½ in) long, oval, with three grooves.

Position: Sunny, south- and west-facing walls.

Soil: Rich in nutrients, permeable. Can be grown in compost in a large container.

Water: In open soil or container, water plentifully during the summer.

Fertilizing: In open soil, two to three times during the summer; every two to three weeks with compound fertilizer in a pot.

Further care: Requires taut wires, strings or sticks as a climbing aid. Pinching out shoot tips encourages branching and formation of flowers. Space plants 60-80 cm (24-32 in) apart.

Use: As a visual screen, for covering a wall or in pots on a balcony.

Runner beans are at once both decorative and useful.

Nasturtiums will flower all summer long.

Runner bean
Phasaeolus coccineus

Annual winding plant, up to 4 m (13 ft) tall. The leaves are soft and feathered, with three lobes.
Origin: South America.
Flower/fruit: Red flower, from early summer to mid-autumn. Green bean pods, up to 30 cm (12 in) long from mid-summer to late autumn. Seeds pink to violet, edible.
Position: Sunny to semi-shady; south- and west-facing walls.
Soil: Deep, rich in nutrients. Use fertilized

standard compost in a large container.
Water: Water plentifully during the summer; when the weather is very dry, water daily both in large containers and open soil.
Fertilizing: Three times during the growing period, using compound fertilizer. In a large container, every six to eight weeks with compound fertilizer.
Further care: Will require a climbing aid such as wire, a stick or string. Space plants 25-30 cm (10-12 in) apart.
Use: Young beans for soups, salads, as a vegetable.
Warning: Green beans are toxic if eaten raw.

Nasturtium
Tropaeolum

Plant with tendrils and large, long-stalked leaves (up to 8 cm/3¼ in across). Hybrids of *T. majus* and *T. peregrinum* are sold.
Origin: South America.
Flower/fruit: *T. majus* has yellow to carmine red flowers from early summer to mid-autumn. Fruit: up to 2 cm (¾ in), light green to yellow, ridged. *T. peregrinum* has very feathery, yellow flowers from mid-summer.
Position: In full sunlight, on south- and west-facing sides of the house.

Soil: Loose, permeable garden soil, or standard compost in a container.
Water: Water plentifully in a large container; in open soil, daily in summer.
Fertilizing: Potassium- and phosphorus-rich fertilizer encourages flower formation. Begin fertilizing when plants in open soil start flowering; every six to eight weeks in a large container.
Further care: Requires a thin grid or wire fence as a climbing aid. Space plants 1 m (40 in) apart.
Diseases: For aphids, spray plants two or three times with tansy brew.
Use: Excellent for covering composting bins or fences.

Ornamental gourds will cover fairly large areas with greenery.

Cucumbers provide fresh ingredients for salads in the summer.

Ornamental gourd
Cucurbita pepo var. *ovifera*

A fast-growing, summer plant with tendrils (up to 8 m/27 ft tall). Leaves 10-20 cm (4-8 in) long; makes a good visual screen. Colourful fruit.
Origin: South America.
Flower/fruit: Mid-summer to mid-autumn; large, funnel-shaped, yellow flowers. Popular with bees. Conspicuous fruit which can be kept for a long time as indoor decoration.
Position: Sunny, south- and west-facing walls.

Soil: Nutrient- and humus-rich soil, best mixed with compost. Use standard compost when growing this plant in a large container.
Water: Plentifully to prevent drying out.
Fertilizing: Every four weeks with compound fertilizer during the vegetative phase in open soil; weekly with liquid fertilizer in a container.
Further care: Requires only a string or other simple climbing aid. Space plants about 2 m (7 ft) apart.
Use: Very good for covering a large area with greenery. Grow on a frame over a compost heap to provide shade.

Cucumber
Cucumis sativus

This plant grows quickly (up to 4 m/13 ft), with green tendrils in summer and large, rough, hairy leaves. Many different varieties.
Origin: Western India.
Flower/fruit: early to late summer, golden yellow flowers 2 cm (¾ in) across with pointed petals. Separate male and female flowers. Popular with bees.
Fruit: A green cucumber.
Position: Sunny, sheltered from wind, south-facing wall.
Soil: Humus- and

nutrient-rich; mixed with compost in a container.
Water: Keep evenly moist. Use water that has been left to stand for a day or more. Dryness will make the fruit bitter.
Fertilizing: In open soil, use diluted, fermented nettle brew two to three times during the vegetation phase (see p. 37) or use compound fertilizer. If grown in a large container, use dissolved compound fertilizer every 21 days.
Further care: It will require strings or a frame to hold on to. (Try builder's concrete reinforcing mesh.) Space plants 1 sq m (3 ft) apart.
Use: For salads.

The flowers of the convolvulous close up at night.

Morning glory needs nutrient-rich, loose soil.

Convolvulous
Convolvulous sepium

 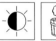

This annual, left-winding plant with arrow-shaped leaves will grow 1-3 m (3-10 ft) tall.
Origin: Central Europe.
Flower/fruit: Late spring to early autumn, white or pink goblet-shaped flowers (5-7 cm/2-2½ in long). The flowers close at night and in bad weather. Fruit: capsule-shaped, pointed, with four to five seeds.
Position: Sunny, west- and east-facing walls.
Soil: Nutrient-rich tending to loamy. In a large container, mix standard compost with some loam.
Water: Keep moist; water well in both open soil and a large container if the weather is dry.
Fertilizing: In open soil, every eight weeks with compound fertilizer during the vegetation phase; every four to six weeks with compound fertilizer if grown in a container.
Further care: Requires a stick, frame or strings for climbing. Otherwise fairly undemanding. Space plants 60-80 cm (24-32 in) apart.
Use: Very picturesque as a covering for a fence.
NB: Contains tannins and resins.

Morning glory
(*Ipomoea tricolor*)

This mainly winding species is fast-growing, up to 5 m (17 ft) tall. Broad, heart-shaped leaves, often with three lobes. Well-known varieties: *I. tricolor* and *I. purpurea*.
Origin: South America.
Flower/fruit: Funnel-shaped single flowers, 10 cm (4 in) across, from mid-summer to early autumn, white with a blue edge. *I. purpurea* has delicate violet flowers. Paper-like, brown fruits, brown seeds.
Position: Warm, sunny and sheltered from wind, south- and west-facing walls.
Soil: Nutrient-rich, loose garden soil with compost; also in large containers.
Water: To protect the soil from drying out, water daily during the summer; twice daily in a container.
Fertilizing: In a large container, once or twice weekly; in open soil, once during the vegetation phase with compound fertilizer.
Further care: Sensitive to wet, cold weather. Spray with tansy brew or pyrethrum preparations as prevention against red spider mites. Space plants 20-25 cm (8-10 in) apart.

Sweet peas come in many varieties.

The flowers are favourites for vases.

Sweet pea

Lathyrus odoratus

This summer-flowering climber can grow up to 2 m (7 ft) tall. Its paired, feathery leaves end in tendrils. The genus includes about ten climbers and also some low-growing species. It is a very popular plant on account of its delicate fragrance and attractive flowers. Many sweet peas flower best during days with many hours of light, which means that, in the autumn, they flower less and less until they finally die. Open-soil varieties and also some for planting in large containers: Cuthbertson sweet peas, Spencer varieties and Zvolaneks Colossals with particularly large flowers on long stalks.

Origin: Southern Europe.
Flower/fruit: mid-summer to mid-autumn, colours range from white through yellow and pink to lavender and deep violet. The flower is delicate and usually has spurs and lateral wings. Strong scent. Fruit: 5-7 cm (2-2¾ in) long pods which turn brown when ripening. They contain spherical seeds.
Position: Warm, sunny and sheltered, cannot cope with draughts. South-facing wall of fence with sufficient shade from the sun. Cannot cope with direct, intense sunlight at midday.
Soil: Nutrient-rich, permeable garden soil. Chalky soil preferred. In a large container, use loose compost.
Water: Keep evenly moist; sensitive to drying out. Cover the soil with mulch. Never allow the planting container to dry out.
Fertilizing: High demand on nutrients. In open soil, water with fermented nettle brew once or twice weekly. Always use organic fertilizer. Use liquid fertilizer once or twice weekly in a large container.
Further care: Will require climbing aids like strings, brushwood, sticks, chicken wire, or a delicate frame as the tendrils cannot cope with very thick supports. Always remove all wilted flowers as soon as possible to ensure continuous flowering. Space plants 15 cm (6 in) apart.
Use: For covering a balcony in greenery, in boxes or pots, on a fence or as a visual screen along the edge of a patio.

My tip: If you cut the flowers early in the morning they will last longer in a vase.

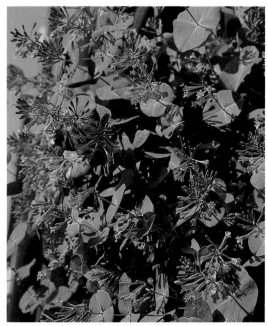

Dutchman's pipe will also grow quite happily in the shade.

The flowers of the honeysuckle spread their strong fragrance in the evening.

Dutchman's pipe
Aristolochia macrophylla

This tall winding plant has conspicuous leaves, 30 cm (12 in) across, that are soft and heart-shaped. It is green throughout the summer and grows up to 10 m (33 ft) high. It will provide a good visual screen with leaves that overlap like roof tiles. Other useful species are *A. moupinensis, A. tomentosa*. This plant is quite happy in a town.
Origin: North America.
Flower/fruit: Late spring to mid-summer, the inconspicuous, small, yellow-green flowers do not appear until about the third to fifth year. They form insect traps. Fruit: a 10 cm (4 in) long capsule.
Position: Shady to semi-shady, north- or east-facing site.
Soil: Loose, nutrient- and humus-rich. Will also cope with chalky soil.
Water: Requires plenty of water; the soil must never be allowed to dry out.
Fertilizing: Young plants two to three times per year with compost and organic fertilizer; older plants twice with compound fertilizer.
Further care: Requires climbing aids. Space plants at 2-3 m (7-10 ft).

Honeysuckle
Lonicera

This vigorously growing winding plant is usually green during the summer and grows 3-6 m (10-20 ft) tall. There are many species.
Origin: Central Europe, western China.
Position: Sunny to semi-shady, south- and west-facing sites.
Soil: Undemanding.
Water: Avoid drying out during the summer, otherwise there is a risk of infestation with aphids.
Fertilizing: Compound fertilizer once a year in open soil; in pots, every four weeks with compound fertilizer.
Further care: Cut back to prevent bareness from below, requires taut wires or sticks as a climbing aid. Space plants 2-3 m (7-10 ft) apart; individual planting preferred.
Overwintering: In large containers with winter protection (see p. 29).
Warning: Toxic berries!
Species:
L. caprifolium: yellow/white flowers
L. heckrottii: reddish flower
L. henryi: red/yellow flowers
L. periclymenum: yellow/white flower
L. tellmaniana: orange flowers

"Lawinia" unfolds large, scented flowers.

"White Cockade" is eminently suitable for displaying in a vase.

Climbing roses
Rosa

Depending on the variety, this makes a 2-5 m (7-17 ft) tall rambling plant. The bush is green during the summer and grows vigorously, with annual shoots up to 5 m (17 ft) long. Its thorns are the actual climbing mechanism of the plant. The leaves are shiny, dark green and slightly serrated. They remain green for a long time in the autumn.
Origin: Crosses from cultivars and from Far-Eastern wild species.

Flower/fruit: Single flowering from late spring to early summer; continuous flowering from early spring to mid-autumn; no flowers until the second year, singly or in bunches, single or double; white, yellow, pink or red flowers with many yellow stamens. Some varieties are scented. Popular with bees. Red, berry-like fruit (hip) from late summer to early autumn with numerous, small, yellow seeds. The fruit can be used to make jam, tea and wine.
Position: Sunny, south- and west-facing sites, sheltered but not too sheltered from wind (not

enough circulation of air will create susceptibility to fungal infections).
Soil: Nutrient-rich, loamy humus.
Water: Plenty during the first year and during drought in open soil; water regularly in large containers. Avoid waterlogging.
Allow the rootstock to soak in a bucket for several hours before planting and water well again after planting. When watering, water the roots but not the leaves.
Fertilizing: Regularly in open soil, from spring to late summer with rose fertilizer. In a large container, every four to six weeks during the

same period.
Further care: Tie shoots to a climbing aid. Cutting out shoots that have finished flowering will encourage continuous flowering roses to produce further flowers. Cut back well in the spring. Space plants 2 m (7 ft) apart.
Diseases/pests: Susceptible to fungal diseases. For prevention and control see page 35.
Overwintering: In open soil, heap up soil around the roots and cover shoots with brushwood or straw. For large container plants, line the pot with polystyrene sheeting and also cover the shoots with straw and tie this in place.

"Golden Showers" flowers continuously.

"Rosenresli" is a robust climbing rose.

Varieties:
Red flowers:

"Flammentanz": blood red, double flowers, flowers once, up to 4 m (13 ft) tall, spreading growth, robust and hardy.

"Gruss an Heidelberg": blood red, double, like cultivated rose, large flowers, scented, continuous flowering, vigorous growth, up to 2 m (7 ft) tall.

"Sympathie": velvety dark red, double, flower like a cultivated rose with strong scent, continuous flowering, up to 3 m (10 ft) tall. Robust variety.

Pink flowers:

"Chaplin's Pink Climber": dark pink, strongly coloured, very large flowers, profusely flowering, semi-double, early flowering. Very vigorous growth, cut off shoots that have finished flowering.

"Coral Dawn": coral pink, double flowers, like cultivated rose, scented, continuous flowering. Up to 3 m (10 ft) tall. Flowers last quite a long time.

"Dorothy Perkins": cherry pink flowers, small, but profusely flowering, scented. Up to 2 m (7 ft) tall.

"Lawinia": pure pink, large double flowers, scented. 2-3 m (7-10 ft) tall. Flowers several times, grows vigorously. Very weather-hardy.

"Rosenresli": To begin with, salmon red, then salmon pink flowers, large, loosely double. Scent of tea roses. Up to 2 m (7 ft) tall. Not susceptible to disease.

Yellow flowers:

"Casino": yellow, large, double flowers, scented, continuous flowering. Up to 2.5 m (8 ft) tall, strong.

"Coupe d'Or": golden yellow, large flowers, profusely flowering, for east- and west-facing walls.

"Golden Showers": lemon yellow, double flower, scented, continuous flowering, up to 2 m (7 ft) tall.

"Goldstern": deep golden-yellow, similar to cultivated roses, double flower, continuous flowering. Up to 2 m (7 ft) tall, robust.

White flowers: "Fräulein Octavia Hesse": pure white flowers, early flowering, vigorous growth, cut shoots sparingly.

"Ilse Krohn Superior": pure white, double, like cultivated rose, continuous flowering, strongly scented, profusely flowering. Up to 2 m (7 ft) tall, robust.

"White Cockade": white, like cultivated rose. Intense scent. Flowers several times, grows vigorously. Good cut flower.

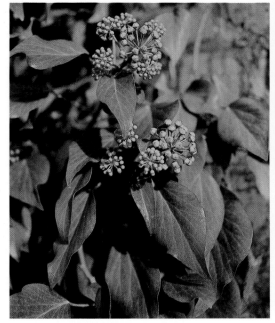

Ivy can live for hundreds of years.

The flower umbels smell faintly of honey.

Ivy
Hedera helix

Ivy is an evergreen climber that can attain heights of up to 30 m (10 ft) with the help of its suckers. It is the only indigenous European plant with root suckers but it can also grow as a ground cover plant in woodland. The leaves of the young plant have three to five lobes, are dark green with white veins and lose the lobes with age. When very old, the shoots of an ivy may be as thick as a human arm. It can live for several hundred years. To begin with, growth is relatively slow. Recommended species include *H. colchica* "Arborescens", with its early flowers, which will attain a height of no more than 1.5 m (60 in); *H. helix* "Goldheart" with small, yellow leaves; *H. hibernica* which has larger leaves than *H. helix*, is more sensitive to frost and rarely produces fruits.

Origin: Central Europe, North Africa, Asia.
Flower/fruit: Early to mid-autumn, inconspicuous, green/yellow, semi-spherical flower umbels that smell faintly of honey. Flowers do not appear until the plant is five to ten years old. The berries are popular with birds.
Position: Semi-shade, shade, north- and east-facing walls. Bright south-facing walls are too hot.
Soil: Humus-rich, slightly sandy, loamy soil; loamy standard compost in large containers.
Water: Water well in a large container and in open soil during dry weather and in the autumn, otherwise keep fairly moist. Ivy loves high humidity, so enjoys the shade of trees.
Fertilizing: Not demanding; one to two doses of compound fertilizer during the vegetative phase in open soil. Every eight to ten weeks in summer give compound fertilizer if grown in a large container.
Further care: Train young plants upwards with the help of a stick. No need to cut back; will cope with a shaping cut. Space plants 1-2 m (3-7 ft) apart.
Use: Eminently suitable for covering undamaged walls and façades.
Overwintering: Give winter protection if in a large container (see p. 29).

My tip: Ivy is a ground-covering plant which will not climb until it meets a vertical obstacle.

Warning: The berries are very toxic!

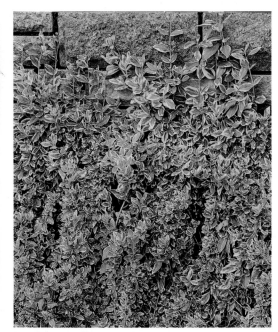

The flowering racemes of wisteria.

Spindleberry will thrive in the shade.

Wisteria
Wisteria sinensis ☠

This is a winding plant that will grow up to 10 m (33 ft) tall, with 1 m (3 ft) long annual shoots and asymmetrical feathered leaves.
Origin: North America, eastern Asia.
Flower/fruit: Mid to late spring, numerous, 15-30 cm (6-12 in) long blue violet racemes at five to ten years. Delicately scented. Occasionally, velvet-haired, 10-20 cm (4-8 in) fruit pods in late spring.
Position: Warm, sunny.

South- and west-facing sites.
Soil: Nutrient-rich, permeable and humus-rich. Hates chalk.
Water: Daily during the summer.
Fertilizing: In open soil, once or twice during the vegetation period with compound fertilizer.
Further care: Requires a stable wire as a climbing aid; cut back after flowering; shortening young shoots during the summer will encourage the formation of lots of flowers. Space plants 2-3 m (7-10 ft) apart; it is better to grow plants individually.
Warning: All parts of this plant are toxic!

Spindleberry
Euonymus fortunei ☠

This evergreen shrub climbs with the help of root suckers and can grow to about 2 m (7 ft) tall. Depending on the species, the foliage is light green, variegated yellow or dark green. The leaves are 2-6 cm (¾-2½ in) across and generally red in winter.
Origin: Eastern Asia.
Flower/fruit: Late spring to early summer, greenish-yellow flowers grouped in umbels. It sometimes produces white fruit with orange

red toxic seeds.
Position: Semi-shade, shady, north- and east-facing sites.
Soil: Humus-rich, loamy, with a high content of lime. In a container, in loamy standard compost.
Water: Water well during the autumn and winter.
Fertilizing: In open soil, two to three times a year with organic fertilizer. In a pot, every six weeks with a compound fertilizer. Further care: Will need a climbing aid. Avoid cutting back as the plant gets older. Space plants 1.5-2 m (5-7 ft) apart.
Overwintering: In a pot with winter protection.
Warning: The seeds are toxic!

The autumn colouring of Parthenocissus tricuspidata ranges from yellow through orange to red.

Virginia creeper
Parthenocissus

A climbing shrub which is green in summer. Some can grow more than 10 m (33 ft) tall without any climbing aid. They anchor themselves to any support, using tendrils that have been converted into adhesive pads. Two species are most common: *P. quinquefolia* and *P. tricuspidata*. Both can cope well with a town or city atmosphere and they are particularly suited to covering large areas of walls and façades with greenery.

Parthenocissus quinquefolia

Fast-growing, 8-12 m (27-40 ft) tall, winding plant, green in summer, with suckers, and sometimes with adhesive pads at the ends of shoots. The leaf is about 12 cm (4¾ in) across, dark green; in autumn an intense carmine red. Also available is *P. quinquefolia* "Engelmanii", 10-12 m (33-40 ft) tall, with adhesive pads at the ends of shoots. Dark red colouring in the autumn.
Origin: North America.
Flower/fruit: In summer, inconspicuous flower, whitish-green, with panicles. Strong pleasant scent, popular with bees.
Fruit: blue pea-sized berries, much sought after by birds.
Position: Sunny to semi-shady. Autumn colour will be better in a sunny position. South-, west- and east-facing sites.
Soil: Humus-rich. Use standard compost in a large container.
Water: Water well during drought in any site.
Fertilizing: In open soil, once a year; every eight weeks with compound fertilizer in a pot.
Further care: Young plants require taut wires or a climbing frame. Space plants 2 m (7 ft) apart.
Overwintering: Give protection if in a pot.

Parthenocissus tricuspidata

May grow up to 10 (15) m (33-50 ft) within one to two years. Self-climbing; the ends of shoots have adhesive pads with which the plant is able to hold on by secreting an adhesive (see p. 9). The leaf has three lobes, is 10-20 cm (4-8 in) wide, bronze coloured when shooting, then deep green and shiny; autumn colouring from yellow to orange to red. The variety *P. tricuspidata* "Veitchii" is widely available in the gardening trade and is distinguishable from *P. tricuspidata* by smaller, more oval leaves with three lobes.

Food for birds: Parthenocissus quinquefolia berries.

The grapevine bears tasty fruit from the first month of autumn onwards.

P. tricuspidata "Veitchii Gigantea" has broad leaves. *P. tricuspidata* "Veitchii Aurea" has yellow green leaves with reddish edges; less vigorous than other varieties.
Origin: Eastern Asia.
Flower/fruit: early to mid-summer, yellowish-green flower, faintly scented, popular with bees. In late summer pea-sized, bluish-black berries ripen on red stalks.
Position: Sunny, semi-shady, south- and west-facing sites.
Soil: Nutrient-rich, deep; use standard compost in a large container.
Water: During a drought, water plants well in large

containers and open soil.
Fertilizing: Undemanding; once or twice annually in open soil. About every four to six weeks with compound fertilizer in a large container.
Further care: *P. tricuspidata* "Veitchii" does not require any climbing aid. It may die back a little due to frost damage but will soon produce new shoots from below. Space plants 2-3 m (7-10 ft) apart.
Overwintering: Give protection to containers.
Use: All forms of *P. tricuspidata* are suited to growing in containers. *P. tricuspidata* "Veitchii" will cover even concrete walls with greenery.

Grapevine
Vitis vinifera

This is a vigorously growing plant with suckers, which grows up to 10 m (33 ft) tall. Its annual shoots can be up to 3 m (10 ft) long. The leaves have three to five lobes, are roundish and change colour in the autumn. For planting in cooler regions, try white or red "Gutedel", "Früher Malinger" and "Früher Blauer Burgunder". Always plant two plants one beside the other.
Origin: Central and south-eastern Europe.

Flower/fruit: Later spring to mid-summer, small, yellowish-green panicles, slightly scented. Fruit from erly autumn; grapes with two to four seeds, light yellow or bluish-red.
Position: Sunny, warm, south-facing site; sheltered from wind.
Soil: Nutrient-rich, sandy, loamy.
Water: Undemanding; protect the soil from drying out.
Fertilizing: As a fruiting vine two to four times annually, with mineral fertilizer.
Further care: Cut back to a few shoots in mid-winter. Space plants 2-5 m (6-17 ft) apart.

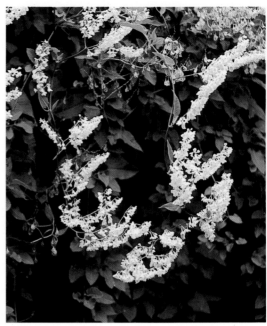

Kiwi fruit requires a warm, sunny position.

Russian vine unfolds delicately scented flowers.

Kiwi fruit, Chinese gooseberry
Actinidia chinensis

This is a fast-growing, left-winding plant, green in summer, 4-8 m (13-27 ft) tall. The leaves are undivided, with serrated edges. Plant both female and male plants to obtain fruit. Suitable for a city climate.
Origin: South-east Asia.
Flower/fruit: During late spring to early summer, white flowers appear, 3-4 cm (1¼ -1½ in) across, pleasantly scented, turning yellow towards the end of the flowering period. The fruit grows to a maximum of 5 cm (2 in), from late summer.
Position: Warm, south-facing.
Soil: Nutrient- and humus-rich with very little lime in open soil; standard compost in a large container.
Water: Never allow the soil to dry out.
Fertilizing: In open soil during the summer, every six weeks with compound fertilizer. In a large container, every month.
Further care: Requires a climbing aid. Cutting back annual shoots encourages more flowers. Space plants 1-2 m (3-7 ft) apart.
Overwintering: Provide winter protection in a pot.

Russian vine
Fallopia baldschuanica

This climber can reach up to 8-15 m (27-50 ft). It is a winding plant. The young leaves are reddish, later light green, and turn yellowish in the autumn, heart-shaped and 4-9 cm (1½-3½ in) long.
Origin: Eastern Asia.
Flower/fruit: Mid-summer to mid-autumn, white, 15-20 cm (6-8 in) long panicles with a slight scent. Popular with bees. Flowers from the second year onward. Fruit: from early autumn, winged brown nut, eaten by birds.
Position: Sunny to semi-shady, south-, west- and east-facing sites.
Soil: Open soil should be humus- and nutrient-rich; standard compost in a large container.
Water: In a large container, daily during the summer; open soil should not be left to dry out.
Fertilizing: In a large container, every second to fourth week until the end of summer. In open soil, twice with annually compound fertilizer.
Further care: Strong climbing aid required. Cut back in spring. Space plants at 2-3 m (7-10 ft).
Overwintering: In a large container provide winter protection (see p. 29).

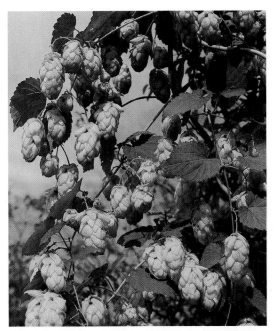

Winter jasmine will begin to flower from the last month of winter onwards.

The fruit of the hop is also much in demand for flower arranging.

Winter jasmine
Jasminum nudiflorum

This rambling plant is green in summer, with bright green leaves and long, arched and trailing shoots. Up to 3 m (10 ft) tall, a lovely early-flowering plant.
Origin: Eastern Asia.
Flower/fruit: Depending on the position, early winter or early spring; star-shaped, yellow flowers, 2.5 cm (1 in) long, after five years. Fruit: rare, black berries.
Position: Sunny to semi-shady, warm, sheltered. South-facing site; west-

facing with protection from wind.
Soil: Permeable, humus-rich.
Water: Water well in autumn before frosts commence, the shoots lose water through evaporation even in winter. Also water well in summer in dry periods.
Fertilizing: Once or twice annually with compound fertilizer.
Further care: Climbing aids required, such as wires or a climbing frame, needs tying. Prune in spring every two to three years. Space plants 2-3 m (7-10 ft) apart.
Use: Its hanging shoots make it an ideal covering for walls and banks.

Hop
Humulus lupulus

This is a 6 m (20 ft) tall, winding plant. The leaves are heart-shaped, up to 15 cm (6 in) across and have three lobes. There are both male and female plants.
H. scandens does not grow as fast nor is it as hardy as *H. lupulus*.
Origin: Central Europe.
Flower/fruit: Mid- to late summer, greenish, female, strongly scented catkins and male flowers in panicles. Fruit: almost cone-shaped, hanging, from early autumn.

Position: Semi-shady, west- and east-facing sites.
Soil: In open soil, nutrient-rich, loamy soil; in a large container, loamy standard compost.
Water: Water well in dry weather. Avoid waterlogging in a large container.
Fertilizing: In open soil, once or twice annually; regularly every six to eight weeks in a large container; with compound fertilizer.
Further care: use a stick or wire as a climbing aid. Cut back in autumn. Space plants 2-2.5 m (7-8 ft) apart.
Overwintering: Provide winter protection in a large container (see p. 29).

Clematis montana "Rubens" will produce an abundance of flowers.

Clematis "Jackmanii" bears enormous star-shaped flowers.

Clematis
Clematis
(wild forms)

Almost exclusively at home in the northern hemisphere. This winding plant has green leaves in summer and climbs up to 10 m (33 ft) high. Less vigorously growing clematis species are suitable for large pots.
Flower/fruit: Late spring to early autumn, bell-like or open flowers singly or in panicles. The wild forms have abundant flowers. Fruit: feathery.
Position: Semi-shady. The area around the roots must be covered by plants; west- and east-facing sites; south-facing with protection from sun.
Soil: Humus-rich, permeable, moist. Can cope with lime; use standard compost in a large container.
Water: On hot summer days, water daily but avoid waterlogging.
Fertilizing: In open soil, once or twice annually; in a container, every six weeks with compound fertilizer until late summer.
Further care: Requires a climbing aid. Plant deep; the rootstock should be at least 10 cm (4 in) beneath the soil. *C. montana, C.* "Lasurstern" and *C.* "The President" should be cut back after flowering. All other clematis should be cut back in early spring. Space plants at 2-3 m (7-10 ft).
Overwintering: Provide winter protection in a large container (see p. 29). Protect from frost when plants are young.

Warning: All species are slightly toxic!

Clematis montana

Grows 6-8 m (20-27 ft) tall; leaves reddish-brown when shooting, later dark green. The wild form is generally not available in the gardening trade, only cultivated varieties. *C. montana* "Rubens" (pink-flowering) or *C. montana* "Superba" (white).
Origin: Central China, Himalayas.
Flower/fruit: Late spring to early summer, white flowers, up to 4 cm (1½ in) across, when the plant is three to five years old; cultivated varieties flower abundantly.

Traveller's joy, old man's beard
Clematis vitalba

This tall-growing wild species grows rapidly to over 20 m (800 in). The oval leaves are up to 10 cm (4 in) long.

Origin: Central Europe.
Flower/fruit: Mid-spring to mid-autumn, white, up to 2 cm (¾ in) across, with slight scent of almonds, produced three to five years after planting. Fruit: from late spring to late winter, silvery seedheads.

Clematis hybrids

The large-flowered cultivars are more suited to growing in large containers. Cultivated clematis varieties have oval leaves 15 cm (6 in) long, and climb to 4 m (13 ft).
Origin: Usually from British and French raisers.
Soil, water, fertilizing and further care: as for wild varieties.
Diseases: Clematis wilt.
"Ernest Markham": flower: mid-summer to early autumn, 10-15 cm (4-6 in), brilliant dark violet.
"Jackmanii": robust and hardy. Flower: mid-summer to mid-autumn, 10-15 cm (4-6 in), abundantly flowering, violet purple.
"Lasurstern": Flower: late spring to early summer; again in early autumn, 10-15 cm (4-6 in), violet blue.
"Nelly Moser": Flower: late spring to early summer, again early autumn, 15-20 cm (6-8 in), pale pink striped.
"The President": Flower: early to mid-summer, again mid-autumn, up to 15 cm (6 in), dark violet.
"Ville de Lyon": Flower: early summer to early autumn, 10-15 cm (4-6 in), deep carmine red.

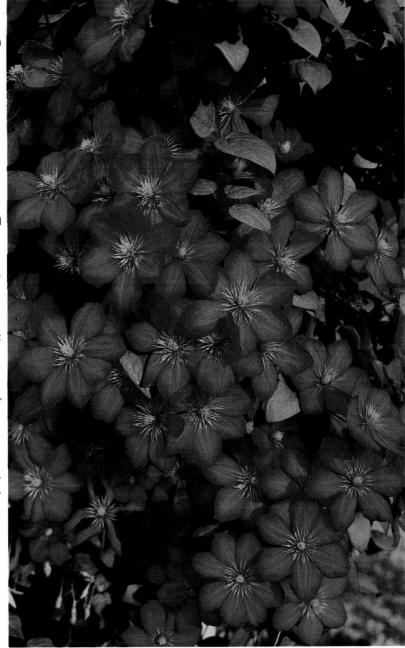

Clematis "Ville de Lyon" forms a thick tapestry of blossom.

Pear flowers are a delight for bees.

Pears will yield lots of fruit on an espalier

Pear
Pyrus communis

The pear is a 15-20 m (50-70 ft) tall, pyramid-shaped, deciduous tree. The pear can only be pollinated with pollen from other pear trees, so several trees must be planted in the same vicinity. The leaves are roundish-oval.

Origin: Central Europe.

Flower/fruit: Mid to late spring, white flowers with petals up to 2.5 cm (1 in) across. Numerous reddish-yellow stamens. Fruit ripens from late summer to late autumn.

Position: Sheltered, sunny, south- or south-west-facing espalier.

Soil: Deep, nutrient-rich, slightly sandy.

Water: Requires sufficient moisture; water well in dry weather but does not like waterlogging.

Fertilizing: Three times with compound fertilizer (in the spring, summer and autumn, see apple, p. 59).

Further care: Do not plant in the vicinity of junipers (risk of pear rust, see p. 35). Space plants 3-7 m (10-23 ft) apart.

Use: Suited to growing as a fan-shaped espalier.

Espalier varieties:

"Alexander Lucas": Flower medium early; large grass green to yellow green fruit, juicy and sweet. Ripens mid-autumn. Storage: until early winter.

"Gute Luise": Flowering time short; fruit: large, green to reddish-yellow, very tasty and juicy. Ripens: early to mid-autumn. Storage: until late autumn. Good yield and fruit quality.

"Mme. Verté": Longlasting flower, good pollen producer; fruit: small, plump, greenish-brown and pleasantly sweet. Ripens: mid-autumn to early winter. Storage: until late winter. Regular yield even in unfavourable positions.

"Napoleon's Butterbirne": Longlasting flower, robust; fruit: medium-sized, bottle-shaped, light green to light yellow, very juicy and a little sharp. Ripens: mid to late autumn. Storage: until early winter. High yield.

"Regentin": The flower is slightly sensitive to frost; fruit: medium sized, whitish-green, juicy and tasty, a wonderful winter pear. Ripens: mid to late autumn. Storage: early to mid-winter.

"Williams Christ": Small, robust flower; fruit: large, yellowish-green, very tasty and tender. Ripens: late summer. Storage: one to two weeks. High nutrient requirements; not quite hardy in frost.

Peach trees bloom as early as the first month of spring. *The first fruit is ripe by the middle of summer.*

Peach
Prunus persica

This deciduous tree, which grows up to 8 m (27 ft) tall, has dark green, longish, serrated leaves. It grows quickly but does not live for very long. Peach trees are self-pollinating so one specimen is sufficient for producing fruit. Bush forms are usually available in the trade. Grown as a cultivated variety as a peach seedling on light, sandy soils; if the soil is heavy and loamy, a peach scion is grafted on to a plum stock.

Origin: Probably China.
Flower/fruit: From early to mid-spring, 1.5-5 cm (½-2 in) long, dark pink petals. Fruit: mid-summer to early autumn, varieties with yellow or white fruit flesh. Roundish, yellow to reddish, velvet-skinned fruit with a large, brown kernel. Recently, smooth-skinned varieties (nectarines) are much cultivated.
Position: sunny, warm and sheltered. South-facing site.
Soil: Sandy but nutrient-rich.
Water: Can cope with short-term lack of water but the soil should not be allowed to dry out.
Fertilizing: Three times

during the vegetation period with compound fertilizer, not too late in the autumn to guarantee maturing of the wood.
Further care: Cut back in early spring. Space plants 3-5 m (10-17 ft) apart.
Varieties:
"Mamie Ross": Flower fairly hardy; fruit: medium-sized, light red, striped, slightly sharp taste. Ripens: late spring-early summer. Storage: up to one week. Will still ripen even in cooler areas.
"Mayflower": Flower, longlasting, early; fruit: small, bright red, striped, greenish-white flesh, velvety skin which pulls off easily. Ripens: mid-summer. Storage: eat

fresh. A resistant early variety.
"Proskauer": Flower small and late, relatively resistant to frost; fruit: medium-sized, flesh yellowish-white, kernel easy to remove, tasty. Ripens: late summer to early autumn. Storage: eat fresh. Will still ripen even in regions with a rough climate.
"Weisser Ellerstädter": flower medium-sized; fruit: large, spherical, yellowish-white with white flesh, kernel easy to remove, tasty. Ripens: early autumn. Storage: eat fresh. Resistant to disease; produces abundant fruit.

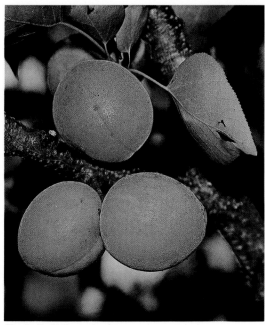

Apricots, like peaches, bloom early.

The tasty fruit can be frozen.

Apricot
Prunus armeniaca

This deciduous tree grows 3-4 m (10-13 ft) tall, in favourable areas even taller. The wild form was originally a tree of the steppes, so it requires plenty of warmth. The leaves are broad, oval to heart-shaped, dark green with slightly serrated edges. Cultivated trees are grafted on to different kinds of stock, the one most frequently used is the root of a plum tree (advantage: smaller growth). Usually available as a shrubby tree in the trade. Apricots are usually self-pollinating, so only one variety is required to harvest fruit.

Origin: Northern China.

Flower/fruit: Mid-spring, medium risk of frost damage, five white petals up to 2 cm (¾ in) long, numerous yellow stamens. Popular with bees. Fruit from mid-summer onwards, orange yellow, roundish with a large, brown kernel, fuzzy skin.

Position: Sunny, dry and sheltered. Apart from really warm areas, only recommended as an espalier on the south-facing side of a house.

Soil: Light, sandy but nutrient-rich.

Water: Prefers a dry climate, sensitive to positions that are too moist and which might encourage infestation by fungal diseases (see p. 35).

Fertilizing: Three times during the vegetation period, with compound fertilizer; no later than early autumn so that maturing of the wood is not delayed.

Further care: In positions that are at risk from late frosts the flowers can be protected from freezing if they are sprayed with water immediately before the onset of the frost, as the water will then freeze on the flower and the flower will be insulated by its coat of ice. Space plants 3-5 m (10-17 ft) apart.

My tip: The fruit is suitable for freezing.

Cultivated varieties: "Grosse, Wahre Frühaprikose" (early, true apricot): Flower sensitive to frost; fruit: large, oval, tasty. Ripens: mid-summer. Storage: eat fresh. Variety with abundant yield.

"Aprikose von Nancy": Flower medium early; fruit: orange yellow to carmine red, sweet with a fine sharp taste; velvety skin. Ripens: mid to late summer. Storage: eat fresh. Relatively hardy to frost, high yielding if given a regular pruning.

Apple blossom is enchantingly beautiful with a delicate scent.

Espalier apples are often sweeter than those from a tree.

Apple
Malus domestica

This deciduous tree has been an indigenous European plant for thousands of years. It is grafted on to various stocks for a high yield of fruit (see p. 33). It grows up to 10 m (33 ft) tall but can also easily be grown as an espalier. Numerous varieties. Apples require pollen from another tree, so try to plant two different varieties side by side.

Origin: Central and south-eastern Europe.
Flower/fruit: From mid to late spring, whitish-pink flowers, pink when still closed, up to 2 cm (¾ in) acrsss, with numerous yellow stamens. Popular with bees. Fruit ripens, depending on variety, from mid-summer to late autumn.
Position: Sunny to semi-shady, east-facing site.
Soil: Nutrient-rich, loose, loamy.
Water: Keep soil moist, protect it from drying out.
Fertilizing: Three times annually with compound fertilizer (spring: for faster growth; summer: growth of fruit; autumn: energy loss through harvest). Fertilizing too late in the autumn will hinder the maturing of the wood!

Also use garden compost as a fertilizer.
Further care: Pruning required (see p. 33). Mulching will prevent washing out of nutrients (use grass cuttings). Space plants 3-5 m (10-17 ft) apart.
Diseases/pests: Guard against mildew by providing a well-ventilated position.
Varieties:
"Berlepsch": flower slightly sensitive to frost; golden yellow fruit, juicy, tasty. Ripens: mid to late autumn. Storage: until late winter; high yield, resistant.
"Cox's Orange": late, longlasting flower; yellow red fruit. Ripens: mid-

autumn. Storage: until late winter. Wood slightly sensitive to frost.
"Goldparmäne": flower not very sensitive to frost; red yellow fruit, sweet, tasty. Ripens: mid-autumn; Storage: until late winter.
"James Grieve": robust flowers; fruit: light yellow to light red, sharp-sweet. Ripens: early to late autumn; Storage: six weeks. Rejuvenating cut required!
"Klarapfel": frost-resistant flower; whitish-yellow, slightly sharp fruit. Ripens: mid to late summer. Storage: three weeks. Disease-resistant variety.

Index

Numbers given in bold indicate illustrations.

Actinidia chinensis 52, **52**
adhesive pads 9
 climbing plants with 9, **9**
adhesive roots 9
air, exchange of 31
aphids 36
apple 59
 varieties:
 "Berlepsch" 59
 "Cox's Orange" 59
 "Goldparmane" 59
 "James Grieve" 59
 "Klarapfel" 59
apricot 58, **58**
 varieties:
 "Aprikose von Nancy" 58
 "True Early Apricot" 58
Aristolochia macrophylla 45, **45**
artificial fertilizer 27

balcony boxes 25
balcony, planting on a 17
basic fertilizer 22, 28
biological plant protection 36
 agent 37
biological wood preservation agent 12
black-eyed Susan **14**, 40, **40**
boggy soil 22
bonemeal 27
branch stumps, treating 34
brushwood 29
builders' steel mesh grid 12

Campanula 40, **40**
chalk deposits 13
clay pots 13
clematis 19, **24**, 35, **38**, 54, **54**, 55, **55**, **cover**
Clematis alpina "Francess Rivis" 18

"Jackmanii" **54**, 55
"Lasurstern" 55
montana 54
"Rubens" **19**, **54**
"Nelly Moser" 55
"The President" 55
"Ville de Lyon" 55, **55**
vitalba 54
clematis, wild forms 54
 wilt 35
climbing aids 6, 9-13
 frames 8, 13
 insulator for 12
 method of 8, **8**
 organs 9
 plants 6, 7, 18, 23, 39
 for large containers 6
Cobaea scandens 40, **40**
coconut fibre rope 11
codling moth 36
comfrey brew, fermented 32, 37
compost 22
 standard 22
composting station 19
compound fertilizer 27
container plants 6, 7, 18, 23
 wooden 13
controlled-release fertilizer 25, 27
convolvulus 40, **40**, 43, **43**
Convolvulus sepium 43, **43**
cordon 30
crown, shape of 34
cucumber 42, **42**
Cucumis sativus 42, **42**
Cucurbita pepo var. *ovifera* 42, **42**
cutting back 29

damage to a façade 15, 16
damaged roots 23
developing fruit 29, 32
direction of growth 29
diseases 8, 34
drainage holes 13, 24
 in a large container **23**, 24

layer 13
dried blood as fertilizer 27
drying out 34
Dutchman's pipe 45, **45**

espalier, fan-shaped 30
 fruit 16
 species of 39
 high 30
 shape of 30
 trees 8
evaporation 15
evergreens 16
Euonymus fortunei 49, **49**

Fallopia aubertii 52, **52**
fern brew 37
fertilizer 27
 organic 27
 solid 27
fertilizing 27-9
 fruit espaliers 32
 mistakes in 29
filter fabric 23, 24
finger test 27
fruit buds 33
fruit espaliers 6, 30-4
 care of 30
 cutting back 33
 fertilizing 32
 fruit species for 30
 planting 30
 positions for 31
 soil for 31
 species for 30
 tying 32
 with a U-shape **31**
fruit formation 29, 32
 ripe 32

germination 26
gourd 42, **42**
grafting 32, 33
grapevine 32, 51, **51**
greenery around a door 17
 window 18
 evergreen 16
 on a façade 15

on drainpipes 18
on fences 19
on patios 18
grid, diagonal 11
growing plants 25
growth aids for espaliers 30
 phase 26, 28, 29

heat traps 21
Hedera helix 48, **48**
hedges 6
hemp rope 11
 string 29
honeysuckle **10**, **24**, 45, **45**, **cover**
hop 53, **53**
 strings 11, 18
horn chips 23, 27
 meal 27
Hortag 24
humidity 15
Humulus lupulus 53, **53**
humus 22

insect damage 36
insulating layer 13
Ipomoea tricolor 43, **43**
iron deficiency 34
irrigation systems 27
ivy **28**, 48, **48**, **cover**

jasmine 53, **53**
Jasminum nudiflorum 53, **53**

kiwi fruit **3**, 52, **52**

Lathyrus odoratus 44, **44**
leaf buds 33
light 7, 21
lime-rich soil 22
liquid fertilizer 27
Lonicera 45, **45**

magnesium deficiency 34
mail order firms 8
main nutrients 27

Index

Malus domestica 59, **59**
mare's tail brew 37
mildew 35, 36
  downy 36
  powdery 35
mineral fertilizer 23, 27
mites 36
morning glory **3**, **25**, 43, **43**
mulching 23

nasturtiums **2**, **14**, 41, **41**
natural stone troughs 14
nettle brew 37
  fermented 32, 37
nitrogen 27, 32
  deficiency 27, 34
nurseries 8
nutrients 26
  composition of 27
  concentration of 27
  deficiency of 34
  ratio of 32

organic fertilizer 27
ornamental gourd **25**, 42,
  42

paint, water-repellent 16
palmette **31**
Parthenocissus 50
  quinquefolia 50, **51**
  tricuspidata 50, **50**
passion flower **37**
peach 57, **57**
  varieties:
  "Mamie Ross" 57
  "Mayflower" 57
  "Proskauer" 57
  "Weisser Ellerstadter" 57
pear 56, **56**
  espalier **35**
  rust 35
  varieties:
  "Alexander Lucas" 56
  "Gute Luise" 56
  "Mme Verte" 56
  "Napoleon's Butterbirne"
  56

"Regentin" 56
"William's Christ" 56
peaty soils 22
pests 8, 36
Phaseolus coccineus 41,
  41
phosphorus 27, 32
  deficiency 34
plant brews 36, 37
  fermented 32, 36, 37
plant containers 13, 14
  with a water reservoir 14
plant protection, biological
  36, 37
planting, correct 233-6
  along walls **22**
  cut 22
  fruit espaliers 30
  hole 18, 22, 23, 32
  woody stands **32**
plants bought with a
  rootstock 7, 22
  healthy 8
  purchasing 6, 8
  toxic 6, 9, 11
  with climbing organs 16
  with root suckers 8, 9, 11
  with tendrils 9
    climbing aids for 9
plastic-coated grids 12
  rope 11
plastic containers 14
polystyrene sheets 29
position 6, 7, 16, 20, 21
  choice of 16, 29, 31
  for fruit espaliers 31
potassium 27, 32
  deficiency 34
pressure-treated wood 12
pricking out 26
protection against frost 29
  against rain 15
  against wind 17, 18, 19
pruning 29, 30, 33
  espalier fruit trees 33
Prunus armeniaca 58, **58**
  persica 57, **57**
pyrethrum 37

Pyrus communis 56, **56**

rainwater 27
rambling plant 8, 11
roof surfaces 16
rope made from natural
  fibre 11
roots 23, 24
  beginnings of 8
  fine 31
  formation of 32
  space for 24
Rosa 46, **46**, 47, **47**
roses, climbing **17**, **25**, 46,
  46, 47, **47**, **cover**
  varieties:
  "Casino" 47
  "Chaplin's Pink Climber"
  47
  "Coral Dawn" 47
  "Coupe d'Or" 47
  "Dorothy Perkins" 47
  "Flammentanz" 47
  "Fraulein Octavia Hesse"
  47
  "Golden Showers" 47, **47**
  "Goldstern" 47
  "Gruss aus Heidelberg"
  47
  "Ilse Krohn Superior" 47
  "Lawinia" **46**, 47
  "Rosenresli" 47, **47**
  "Sympathie" 47
  "White Cockade" **46**, 47
runner bean 41, **41**
Russian vine **25**, 52, **52**
rust 34
  protection from 11

sap, oozing 34
scale insects 36
seed 25
  tray 26
seedlings 33
semi-shade 21
shrubs 6, 19, 20
  toxic 20
soft fruit 20

soil 7, 21, 22
  characteristics 22
  exchange 22
  for fruit espaliers 31
  garden 22
  improvement 20, 22, 23
  sandy 22
  types 21, 22
sooty mould 35
sowing out 25
sowing seed in a seed tray
  26
spacing between plants 26
spindleberry **24**, 49, **49**
spring pruning 33
stable manure 22
straw 29
strings made of natural
  fibre 11
suckers 9
sulphur preparations 37
summer flowers 6, 7
support sticks 23
sweet pea 44, **44**

tansy brew 37
temperature 7, 21
  balance 15
thinning out cut **33**, 34
Thunbergia alata 40, **40**
topsoil 23
toxic plants 6, 9, 11, 20
trace elements 27
training cut 34
Tropaeolum 41, **41**
trumpet vine **36**
twine 29
tying up 29, 30
  fruit espaliers 32

vegetation period 27, 28
Virginia creeper 50, **50**
Vitis vinifera 51, **51**

wall hooks 12, 18
  spacers 9
water 7, 21
watering 26, 27, 32

gulley for 23
waterlogging 13, 24, 32,
  33
winding plants **5**, 8, 9, **16**,
  17, **21**, **28**, 50, **50**, **51**,
  covers
  climbing aids for 9
  with adapted leaf stalks
    8, 9
winter jasmine 53, **53**
  protection 24, 29
wire mesh grid 12, **13**, 35
wire, plastic-coated 29
  ropes 11
  stretcher 12
wisteria **7**, 49, **49**
wood, formation of 32
  maturity of 32, **32**
  pressure-treated 12
  protection 12
    agents 12
wooden frames 12, 13
woody plants 7
  planting **32**
worms in fruit 36
wound-sealing agent 33

Cover photographs
Front cover: *Clematis.*
Inside front cover: *A wall covered in different types of climbing roses.*
Inside back cover: *Virginia creeper with autumn foliage.*
Back cover: *Virginia creeper (top), honeysuckle (bottom left), flowering ivy (bottom right).*

Photographic acknowledgements
Apel: p. 7; Burda/mein schöner Garten: p. 17, 21, 37; Busek: p. 2, 14 top, 44 right, 51 right; CD-Photo: p. 49 left; Gruner & Jahr: p. 5; Kögel: p. 24 left, 24 centre; Kordes: p. 47 right; Reinhard: p. 3 top, 10, 14 bottom, 40 right, 41, 42 left, 44 left, 46 left, 53 right, 56 left, 59 left, inside front cover; Riedmiller:p. 45 left, 59 right; Sammer: p. 25 centre, 42 right, 43 left, 48 right, 50, 53 left, back cover bottom left; Scherz: p. 3 bottom, 16, 25 left, 28, 35, 36, 43 right, 51 left, 52 right, 56 right, inside back cover, back cover top, bottom right; Schneiders: p. 57 left; Schrempp: p. 58; Seidl: p. 18, 19, 45 right, 48 left, 49 right; Strauss: front cover, 24 right, 25 right, 38, 40 left, 47 left, 54, 55; Wetterwald: p. 46 right, 52 left, 57 right.

This edition published 1995 by Merehurst Limited,
Ferry House, 51-57 Lacy Road,
Putney, London SW15 1PR

© 1992 Gräfe und Unzer GmbH, Munich

ISBN 1 85391 528 9

A catalogue record for this book is available from the British Library.

English text copyright © Merehurst Limited 1995
Translated by Astrid Mick
Edited by Lesley Young
Design and typesetting by Paul Cooper
Printed in Hong Kong by Wing King Tong